A. P. Harrington

Judo Black Belt 2nd Dan of Kodokan, Tokyo
Former Secretary, British Register and Council of Black Belts
Association Limited

Defend Yourself with Karate

Illustrated by Fred Thompson

ARROW BOOKS

ARROW BOOKS LTD
3 Fitzroy Square, London W1

AN IMPRINT OF THE HUTCHINSON GROUP

London Melbourne Sydney Auckland
Wellington Johannesburg Cape Town
and agencies throughout the world

❊

First published by
Stanley Paul & Co. Ltd 1970
Arrow edition 1971

*Made and printed in Great Britain
by The Anchor Press Ltd,
Tiptree, Essex*

ISBN 0 09 905500 4

DEFEND YOURSELF WITH KARATE

*

Karate is one of the most effective forms of self-defence in the world. And it is a method that can be learned by anyone and used by anyone.

Defend Yourself with Karate is a basic instruction manual for the beginner—for men and women. It assumes no previous knowledge nor a high degree of physical fitness. The techniques are simply and clearly described. They can be practised at home. Learn Karate this way and you will become an expert in self-defence.

But in addition, you will discover, or recapture, the pleasures of physical fitness and the improvement to both mental and physical health that follows.

No equipment is needed—only a short amount of time each day.

Fred Thompson has illustrated the text with over ninety exceptionally clear explanatory drawings. The result: an ideal guide for novice and expert.

Acknowledgements

I wish to thank my good friend Fred Thompson, Director of Thompson Artists Ltd, for the brilliant explanatory drawings which he has once again provided.

My thanks are also offered to Tom Leahy for his photography and to John Caskey for his help in demonstrating the Karate technique.

I also wish to express my appreciation to my teachers in Karate and notably to the former All Japan Karate Champion Sensei Keinosuke Enoeda (Black Belt 5th Dan) for his invaluable tuition. The magnificent style and rare teaching ability of this great Champion will certainly improve the standard of Karate throughout Great Britain.

A. P. HARRINGTON

Contents

Illustrations

Introduction

Karate, a martial art, is one of the most effective systems of unarmed defence against unprovoked attack. It is also a most efficient and energetic form of exercise calculated to increase such attributes as patience, strength, suppleness and the quickening of mental reactions for the person who regularly engages in practising the art.

The aim of this book is to offer a realistic form of defence and counter-attack which will nullify unwarranted attacks by others and at the same time provide the reader with a valuable form of exercise for maintaining a vigorous and athletic figure.

While defensive moves appear less spectacular than counter-attack technique they are more fundamental to your safety. If even one or two blows from the attacker land on a vulnerable part of your body all the known methods of counter-attack will be of little use to you if you are already incapacitated to some marked degree. In a slightly different context it is like a well-known boxer was reputed to have said when asked to comment about the skill of another. 'He'd be a good boxer—if only he would learn how to dodge some of the punches'.

The technique described in this book is based upon the Shoto-Kan style of Karate which is one of the oldest forms of Karate.

It is vital from the beginning of training that the correct method is followed as otherwise the benefits are diminished. Correct application is essential and powerful movement is of secondary importance until the technique becomes reasonably well accomplished. If one is too keen to instil too much power into movements at an early juncture the technique is never properly utilised to its full potential.

The moves outlined can be performed in a confined space, such as a small room, in the privacy of your own home.

A. P. HARRINGTON

About Karate and the Japanese Martial Arts

Kara literally translated means Empty while te means Hand so Karate can loosely be interpreted as a method of fighting with 'empty hands'—without weapons.

There are many seemingly authoritative, yet conflicting accounts of when, where and how Karate originated. Some say it originated in China, others Okinawa and yet others Japan. At the present time various forms of Karate are indeed practised in each of these countries now variously credited with the inception of this fighting system.

In the northern provinces of China and Korea the legs seem to play a much greater role than the arms in attacking and defending, whereas the proportion seems to be much more equally balanced in the styles favoured by people in southern China and Japan. In the case of China I have heard the theory propounded that this is due to the fact that the Karatemen of North China are generally taller than their counterparts from the south and therefore they utilise their relatively longer legs much more in Karate.

The most plausible beginning of Karate, judging by the present evidence, would seem to be 17th-century Okinawa. The story is told that the Islanders were forbidden, upon pain of death, to carry weapons when conquered in feudal times, and they devised this system of fighting without weapons in order to afford some protection for themselves against their enemies. This would seem to accord with the utterly utilitarian nature of Karate.

Karate subsequently found its way to Japan where the Japanese quickly assimilated the essentials and possibly improved the system over the succeeding centuries.

During the emergence of Japan into modern times many of the precepts of the ancient codes governing the Samurai were influenced by Buddhist thinking and therefore the 'Knightly arts' become 'ways' to spiritual enlightenment. During this time Ken-do became the way of the sword, Aiki-do the way of harmony, Ju-do the way of gentleness and Karate has often the additive of 'do' signifying that it too is accepted as one of the 'ways'. Indeed in the case of Aiki-do, which was the jealously guarded secret of one or two noble families in Japan for many generations, the 'win-lose' motivation has no special significance. The feeling of competition, which is the basis of all other combative-type activities, is largely replaced by a spirit of co-operation until mastery of technique is gained.

There is little doubt in my mind that Karate is probably the most primitive fighting art in the world today. After studying other methods of combative sports I think that Karate is perhaps the most formidable method of fighting by using parts of the body, yet developed, although like all things of human origin it is not infallible.

For those who wish to acquire an exceptional form of self defence, with limited time at their disposal, there is no other system which compares with Karate. For this reason some techniques of Karate are ideal for a woman to learn as a safeguard for the odd occasion when her natural caution is unable to prevent a physically dangerous situation from developing.

It is as well here to clear up some general misconceptions about Karate. The Japanese method of training for the Karatemen is quite spartan in its physical intensity and from the very outset the toughening of body and mind are given priority.

If an obviously fit young man is not sufficiently keen to exert his capacities to the limit in this extremely hard form of training he is asked to put more effort into his actions and if he still does not he is told to leave the area of instruction. He is, however, quite at liberty to return on the next training session with no hard feelings!

Japanese teachers sometimes deal an advanced pupil an unexpected blow. This is to instil mental control in the pupil and at the same time create a gradual toughening process of his body. For similar reasons the teacher may also speak somewhat sharply to a pupil to see if he reacts by becoming annoyed.

While a few training schools practise breaking things like tiles and pieces of wood with parts of their body this is not usual. Television and films have possibly misled people by flourishing this part of Karate to titillate or enliven a boring production.

In ancient times I believe that a solid ridge of bonelike substance was formed at the knuckles by the simple, but no doubt very painful, expedient of continuously smashing the knuckles against something hard so that callus was constantly becoming formed while the broken bones healed. This is hardly recommendable!

The Karate Union of Great Britain is an association devoted to the furtherance of Karate upon sound ethical lines throughout Great Britain.

I am sure that the Secretary of the K.U.G.B. will be glad to forward the address of a club nearest to your home provided you enclose a stamped addressed envelope with your request—Secretary, T. Heaton Esq., 38 Symons Street, Hr. Broughton, Salford, 7.

By learning Karate one gets a 'great' form of defence which in turn involves a great responsibility to other people. For this reason the following 'statement of intent' is included in every grading record book issued by the K.U.G.B. This solemn undertaking must be adhered to under all circumstances.

'I promise to uphold the true spirit of Karate-Do and never to use the skills that I am taught against any persons, except for the defence of myself, family or friends in the instance of extreme danger or unprovoked attack, or in support of law and order.'

Signed......................

Important Note

You will see from the illustrations that no jackets have been worn by my friend and myself.

I have considered this the best way to demonstrate technique involving the upper body and arms without obscuring these actions by the usually loose-fitting jacket which is worn when practising Karate.

Physical Exercises

The practical application of Karate requires a supple yet strong body, and for this reason I recommend certain exercises which when practised regularly are calculated to improve mobility while helping to strengthen the body. It is important, before practising the defensive moves outlined in this book, that you run through some of the following exercises, for say ten minutes, in order to prepare yourself in advance for every practice session in order that you avoid the real risk of strain which may otherwise result. If you can accomplish the moves in the warm atmosphere of a heated room during cold weather so much the better as this will be a definite aid in promoting elasticity in your joints.

I have limited the number of exercises which require the help of a partner in case this is not practical.

1st Exercise

Stand with your slightly bent legs pressed closely together. Place your hands on their respective knee caps and begin to pivot from your hips and knees in an anti-clockwise circular direction without allowing your feet to move. After a few dozen complete circular revolutions reverse your actions by pivoting your hips and knees to a circular clockwise direction (Fig. 1).

2nd Exercise

This activity is very useful for promoting the power of your grip which is, of course, very important to the Karate-man.

Stand upright with your feet spaced about a yard apart then turn your toes outward as you slightly bend your legs.

17

FIG. I

Extend your arms forward in line with your shoulders and begin to clench your hands to form fists. The aim is to clench and unclench your hands as quickly and as powerfully as possible with the proviso that your hands are properly tightened to form compact fists upon each occasion (Fig. 2).

You should aim to condense as many clutching motions of your hands in about three minutes as possible.

It is imperative that your arms are not bent as otherwise the benefits of the exercise are diminished.

3rd Exercise

'Push-ups' are a very well-known form of exercise for strengthening the arms and shoulder regions. In this modification the emphasis is placed upon tightening the formation of your hands into fists.

Kneel down upon the floor and clench your hands to

FIG. 2

form them into fists. Do this by folding the fingers across the palms of your hands so that the first knuckles of your fingers press into the heel of your hand. Now fold your thumbs inwards so that the inside part of your thumbs are pressed closely into contact with your fore and middle fingers between the first and second knuckles of these fingers (Fig. 3). Now lean forward to the floor and press your clenched fists upon the surface as you support the rest of your weight upon the toes of your feet while raising your knees from the surface (Fig. 4).

The exercise entails you bending and straightening your arms some ten times while supporting the whole of your body weight upon your clenched fists and feet. Once you

FIG. 3

have completed nine 'push-ups' in this fashion hold your
final position for some few seconds on the tenth repetition
so that the front of your body is some few inches from the
surface.

For the older mature man, or lady, a relative amount of
benefit may be derived by supporting the body on the knees

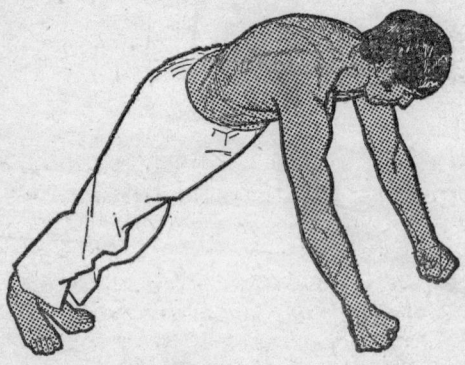

FIG. 4

and fists rather than on the feet and fists. This will entail
less body weight being supported by the arms but will,
nevertheless, be sufficient to make the fists become solidly
formed.

4th Exercise

This activity is a most useful way of exercising the lumbar
region of the body as it entails a vast range of movement
which stretches the body to its limit.

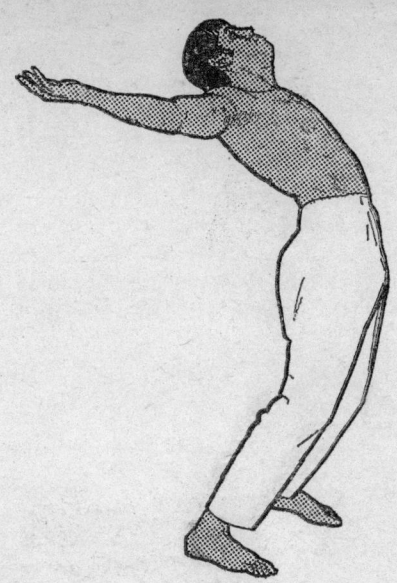

FIG. 5

Start by standing upright with the feet about two yards apart with your extended arms stretched upwards with the palms of the hands facing forward some two yards apart. In effect your body should conform to the letter X. Now without allowing your legs to bend lower your upper body forward as you bring your hands between your feet until you can touch the surface beyond the back of your heels. Continue by straightening your body upwards and then backwards and outwards as you continue by leaning backwards until you can look upwards to the ceiling (Fig. 5). Press your arms backward from this awkward position as you arch your back for a moment or so until you repeat the exercise by once again stretching the upper body forward.

After some few repetitions relax the body.

5th Exercise

Lie down with your back upon the surface and with legs

21

outstretched, position your legs closely together. Clasp your hands together behind your head at the nape of your neck. Raise your legs slowly from the surface and continue raising them until your feet near the ground beyond the crown of your head. At this juncture your stomach muscles will be as relaxed as possible.

Continue your actions by lowering your legs to the floor and just before your heels touch the surface momentarily still your movements before once again raising your legs until your feet near the floor beyond your head.

The exercise is devised to strengthen the stomach muscles

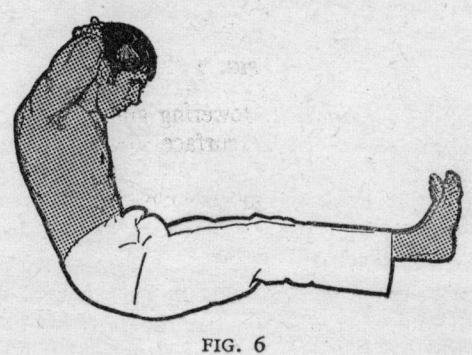

FIG. 6

by not allowing your feet to touch the surface when you lower your legs forward (Fig. 6). You should alternate between having your body outstretched and then bent double some twenty times upon each occasion that you practise the activity.

6th Exercise

Sit down upon the floor then well bend your legs and press the soles of your feet together. Grip your feet with your hands before lowering the outside part of your legs toward the surface. Endeavour to touch the outside part of your knees upon the floor before once again raising your knees from the surface (Fig. 7).

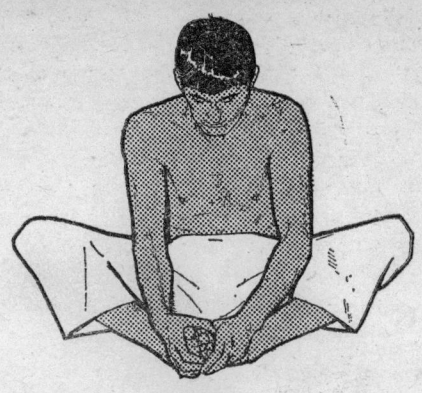

FIG. 7

The activity consists in lowering and raising the upper part of your legs from the surface some twenty or thirty times.

Provided your feet are kept as close as possible to your crutch the exercise is most useful for preserving or aiding elasticity in the knee and hip joints.

7th Exercise

Stand with your feet widely spaced apart and then upraise your arms above their respective shoulders as you lean slightly backwards. Begin to swing your hands and arms around in an anti-clockwise circular direction. As your hands near the ground by your left foot lower your upper body forward and progress by swinging your arms to the right before straightening your upper body once again and then lean slightly backwards as your arms traverse past your right side (Fig. 8). After many anti-clockwise circular actions reverse your movements by swinging your arms round in a large clockwise action as you lower your upper body forward and then straighten yourself and lean backwards.

The activity consists of swaying your body around to follow your arms.

FIG. 8

8th Exercise

Lie down upon the floor with your left flank mostly upon the surface and support yourself on your left forearm. Bend your right leg in such a way that it is positioned upon the surface behind you with your right foot behind your right buttock. Keeping your right shoulder held back swing your right leg round in an anti-clockwise direction and kick with your right foot to the general direction beyond your left side so that the little toe of your right foot is kept uppermost throughout (Fig. 9). Swing your right leg back to its

24

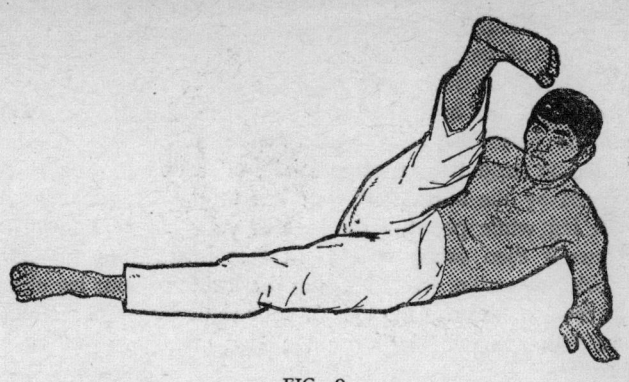

FIG. 9

original position and again make the kicking motion with your right leg.

After you have made some ten kicking motions with your right leg reverse movements where required so that you can accord equal benefit to your left leg. Remember to restrict the movement of your left shoulder in this case so that your left leg is thoroughly exercised.

9th Exercise

Lie down with your back resting upon the floor with legs apart and clear of the surface. Bend your right leg and then powerfully straighten your leg diagonally forward just clear of the floor in a kicking action with the heel part of your foot leading. Continue by bending your left leg before similarly kicking with your left leg by straightening it diagonally forward slightly to the left (Fig. 10). The activity consists of bending and straightening each leg alternately in powerful kicking actions some ten or twenty times.

10th Exercise

It is very important that an exercise is performed for developing ability in moving the legs through a great range of movement.

You should sit down with your legs together outstretched in front of you. Move your straight left leg outwards to your left away from your right leg. Move your right leg to your right and bend the leg so that the inside of your right foot is positioned on the mat behind your right buttock. You can support yourself partially on your left hand positioned by the outside of your left thigh. Straighten your left leg while pressing the toes of your left foot towards yourself then swing your right foot forward in an anti-clockwise action, while keeping the inside of your leg close to the ground until the toes of your right foot almost touch the inside part of your left ankle (Fig. 11). Move your right

FIG. 10

foot back and bend the right leg as your right foot nears your right buttock. Again swing your right leg forward and inwards.

Accomplish this activity say ten times.

Revert to your starting position with legs together in front of yourself. Take your straightened right leg outwards and bring toes toward yourself before swinging your left leg backwards to your left as you bend your left leg when your left foot comes to rest on the mat behind your left buttock. You swing your left leg forward as you keep your right leg straight with your foot arched and stop the actions when the toes of your left foot near the inside of your right ankle. You swing your left leg backward and then forward once again. Do this ten times.

FIG. 11

11th Exercise

Stand upright and support your body weight solely upon your left foot. Raise your right leg from the floor and fully bend your right leg until your right heel is near your crutch. Grasp your right ankle with your left hand and front of your right leg with your right hand (Fig. 12). Suddenly release your grips upon your lower right leg and outstretch your right leg directly to your right in such a way that your leg is straightened until it is parallel to the floor with the sole of your foot facing to your right with the little toe uppermost. Try the same action by moving your left leg sideways to your left.

At first you will probably find this to be a most awkward action and for this reason the number of repetitions should be limited to five for each leg.

After practising the activity on a number of separate occasions gradually instil more power into your leg actions so that the leg is straightened at speed and you utilise a spring-like kicking action. Even when you become well

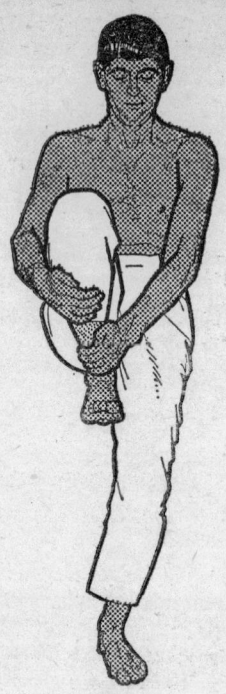

FIG. 12

versed in the required actions you should be very careful to ensure that your kicking actions are not too powerful and that you still limit the number of repetitions.

12th Exercise

Lie down with your back upon the ground and legs bent. Raise your right foot from the floor and then slightly straighten your right leg as though you are kicking an imaginary spot in the air, some two feet above your stomach. As you perform this kicking action bring the toes of your foot toward yourself and imagine that you are using the ball of your foot as the point of contact (Fig. 13).

28

Once you have become used to the required actions gradually increase the speed of your leg actions until you flex and straighten your leg at great speed.

After some two minutes lower your right foot to the floor and repeat the kicking actions with your left leg but remember to start with slow kicking motions at first until the knee joint is 'warmed-up'.

FIG. 13

13th Exercise

Stand upright with your feet just over a yard apart. Slightly bend your legs then turn your toes inwards. Ensure that your toes continue to remain pointed inwards but twist your knees outwards as you hold each side of your belt or place your hands upon their respective hips. This is the stance known as KIBA-DACHI.

Maintain your weight upon your left leg and then flick your right foot inwards and upwards until it nears the inside of part of your upper left thigh (Fig. 14). Quickly replace your right foot upon the floor and then flick your left foot inward and upward until it nears the inside part of your upper right thigh. Continue these actions with your right foot and left foot alternately for some two minutes.

It is essential for the maximum amount of benefit to be derived that you do not straighten your body to ease the facility with which you flick each foot inward and upward. The more difficult this is purposely made by exactly re-

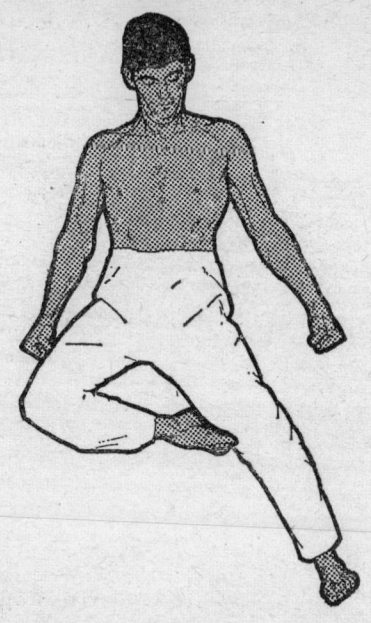

FIG. 14

placing your foot inwards on the ground, while twisting the knees outwards, the better.

14th Exercise

Sit down upon the floor with your legs positioned closely together and outstretched in front of you. Clench both of your hands to form them into fists in the prescribed Karate manner. This is to clench the hands in such a way that the

30

first knuckles of your fingers press closely into the heel of your hand before your thumbs are folded inwards so that the inside part of your thumbs are pressed tightly into contact with the forefingers and middle (index) fingers of your hands between the first and middle knuckles of these fingers. Withdraw your right fist back to your right hip with the palm of the hand uppermost. Keep your right elbow closely pressed into your right side with the little finger edge of your right wrist tightly pressed into your right side.

FIG. 15

Straighten your left arm forward as you raise your straightened legs from the floor until they form roughly a 45-degree angle with the surface when your body will conform almost to the letter V.

Now maintain your posture as you punch forward with your right hand by twisting your thumb inwards just before your right arm becomes fully extended so that your knuckles become twisted uppermost. As you accomplish this arm action you must withdraw your left fist to your left hip with palm uppermost and little finger edge of your left wrist pressed into your left side (Fig. 15). Continue by straightening your left arm and just before the arm becomes straight twist your thumb inwards so that the

31

knuckles of your fist become uppermost. Simultaneously withdraw your right fist to your right hip palm uppermost.

You should continue quick and powerful punching actions, while keeping your legs clear of the floor for a minute or two. Quite apart from the useful exertion of the stomach which is called for this a very good way for training yourself to utilise the stomach when delivering a blow.

Ladies should merely sit upon the floor when practising this technique.

15th Exercise

This exercise is very useful for loosening the shoulder joints before you engage in practising punching actions. Stand with your feet shoulder width apart then swing both arms speedily forward in large circular windmill-like actions. After you have completed some twenty complete revolutions with your arms accomplish an equivalent number by swinging your arms backward.

16th Exercise

This exercise is used in Karate to develop skill in Side Kick (YOKO-GERI).

Lie with your left side on the floor resting on your left forearm facing to your left. Raise your right leg from the surface and ensure that the toes of your foot point toward your left with the big toe nearest to the surface. Well bend your right leg, so that your right foot nears your left knee, then straighten your right leg so that you kick upwards with your little toe nearest you and the sole of your foot uppermost (Fig. 16). After some five kicking actions with your right leg roll over on to your right side and carry out the same form of kicking actions with your left leg.

17th Exercise

You will need the assistance of a partner when practising this activity.

Stand back to back with your partner and link arms. You then sit down slowly while still keeping arms linked. Your

FIG. 16

partner bends his legs then presses backwards upon your back with his as he thrusts the soles of his feet into the floor and begins to raise himself. You resist his actions as much

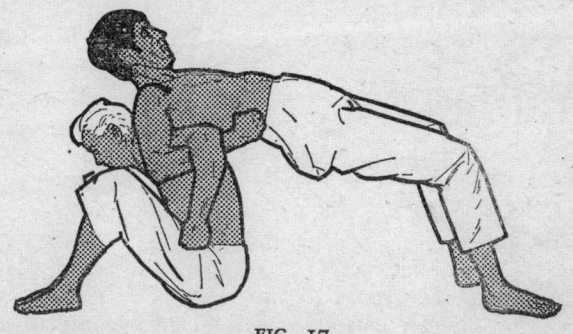

FIG. 17

as possible by using the muscles of your stomach and back. At the same time you must ensure that your legs remain outstretched along the mat with toes pointed upwards. After say three or four seconds your partner relaxes his pressure and you then bend your legs and force your back backwards into his (Fig. 17).

Do this some five times each upon every occasion you exercise at the end of each session, but be careful not to cause hurt to one another by using too much force in the initial stages of training.

18th Exercise

This exercise calls for the assistance of a partner.

You stand facing your partner some three feet apart. Supporting your weight upon your bent left leg twist to

FIG. 18

your right and raise your right foot from the floor. Continue by placing the sole of your right foot into your partner's stomach with toes pointing to his right and the little toe uppermost so that your foot is parallel to the surface of the floor.

Ask your partner to grip your right ankle with both hands before gradually pulling at your ankle. You resist by holding yourself back while keeping your weight securely poised over your left leg (Fig. 18). After some twenty seconds revert by replacing your right foot to the floor before twisting to your right and upraising your left foot. When your left foot nears your partner's stomach he again grips the ankle while making certain that your left foot is made to turn fully inward before exerting a pulling pressure upon your left leg at the ankle.

After you have accomplished the exercise with both your right and left leg three times your partner should then upraise his right leg so that you grip his right ankle, and you reverse roles so that he can practise the actions.

19th Exercise

Fully bend both legs then outstretch your left leg directly to your left with the back of your left heel upon the floor. Place your hands upon your left knee cap and exert a reasonable amount of spasmodic downward pressure upon your knee joint as you very slightly jog up and down upon your right foot while keeping your right leg almost fully bent (Fig. 19).

FIG. 19

After a minute or so of exercising your left leg reverse your movements where required so that you can give an equal amount of benefit to your right leg.

20th Exercise
Sit down upon the floor then lower the inside of your right leg to the surface behind you so that your right foot is close to your right buttock. Partially straighten your left leg forward in front of you with the outside part of your left leg upon the floor. Raise your lightly clenched hands in

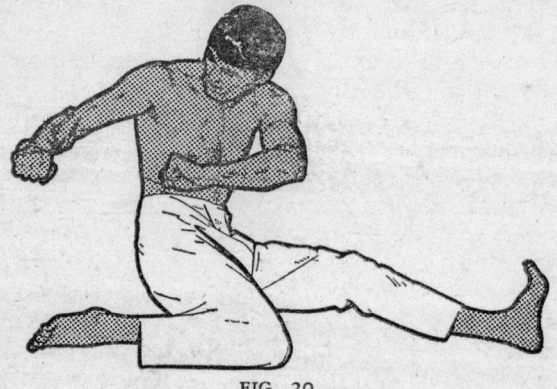

FIG. 20

front of your chest, some few inches apart, before twisting reasonably sharply from the hips until you look towards your rear. Do this some ten times (Fig. 20).

Swing your legs round until your right leg is in front of you and your bent left leg is behind you, then twist sharply to your left.

'The Blocks'

In the Karate style of fighting the parts of your body mainly used for defence are the edges of your wrists and lower forearms. If a useful working knowledge of the basic forms of blocking methods which I recommend are clearly understood, and able to be properly utilised, there is little danger of suffering harm from the normal run of unarmed hooligan.

In my opinion it is important not to enlarge the complexity of the subject by learning too many defensive forms unless you intend to devote a very considerable amount of time and effort to the acquisition of expertise in the art.

The aim is to protect your body, from the knees upwards to the top of your head, by using the lower arms to knock the attackers' limb aside. It is essential that the blocking action of your arm is stilled once the attacker's hand, elbow, knee or foot is diverted from hitting your body. If your actions continue for too long your blocking arm will be too far away to be used quickly for a further blocking action or counter-attack.

Within the precepts of effectiveness and safety you should aim usually to move your lower arm to a great degree just before blocking the attacker in order to develop the correct technique and power. When you use the blocking action in the forearm you must always use a twisting action of your hand which in turn twists the whole lower arm from the elbow to the hand. This vital twisting action generates enormous power into the blocking action and impels the attacking limb away from its target.

In order to acclimatise yourself safely to nullify an attacker's blows it is best to learn the blocks, which are described in four stages. At first you ought to practise the actions in slow motion in front of a large mirror while concentrating on acquiring the technique. After gaining the necessary skill you add more power to your movements. You then try the blocks out while moving about the room or wherever you happen to be practising.

Lastly you try out the defensive blocks on the move with a partner. At the final stage you can use a reasonable amount of power which might entail a toughening process of the forearm region due to the powerful form of contact. If this is not thought wise, and I do not think it is vital, you can both wear padding at the forearm and wrists to prevent discomfort during continuous blocking. After all, one would not expect to block for more than a few times under combat conditions. This might not be the case, however, where one would wish to study the art over a considerable period of time.

Downward Block

I recommend the implementation of this particular block as the preliminary move, wherever possible, if you are in danger of attack. It has the distinct advantage of pre-supposing that the attacker suddenly lashes out with his right foot aimed at your stomach and at the same time it is an admirable stance to adopt when generally defending yourself or counter-attacking. I think it is the best basic posture to use under a variety of different conditions.

While the blocking action must, of course, be learnt on both sides it is wise to keep the particular 'fighting stance' of the left side blocking action which is given first as your usual stance. If too much latitude is introduced in this respect it does tend to diminish the effectiveness of habitual defensive and counter-attacking moves without an equal amount of benefit being gained by the surprise of changing sides, as it were.

The difficulty of learning this technique is that one has both to block at speed while assuming a firmly balanced stance. Because of this I have thought it best to describe the technique in some detail. Let us deal with the movement of your legs and body at first before considering the actual movement of the arms which in reality takes place simultaneously.

Stand upright with your feet pointing directly forward about shoulder width apart. Support your weight upon your left leg as you glide your right foot inwards toward your left foot. When your right foot nears your left foot change its direction by moving it diagonally backwards to the right and place your foot, turned slightly to your right, upon the floor some twenty or so inches behind the point where it was originally positioned. Now straighten your right leg so that it becomes braced back behind you. As this action is accomplished you should slightly pivot inwards on your left foot so that the toes point to the same general direction as your right foot points when you well bend your left leg before twisting your left knee outwards. On no account should you have the impression that you are lightly poised in this position but instead sink your weight so that you become 'rooted' to the floor.

There are four main points to bear in mind. Your left knee must be twisted outwards, although this is not a natural movement, as otherwise it is very easy for a potential attacker to pull you off balance. Your right foot must not be turned outwards to your right too much as otherwise it would tend to retard your speed of retreat. Your back must be kept straight with your hips pushed powerfully forward and the muscles of your right thigh and loins. caused to become tensed. Your heels must be kept planted firmly upon the floor.

Once you have gained some practical experience in the movements involving the legs and body for this technique you will be ready to progress by incorporating the necessary arm actions.

Stand upright with feet shoulder width apart and clench your hands to form fists in the prescribed way. Raise your straightened right arm in front of you until it is parallel to the floor with the right fist pointing at the imaginary attacker. Bend your left arm before traversing your left fist diagonally across your body to over your outstretched right arm. Twist your left clenched hand so that the palm of your hand is able to be brought close to your right cheek with the edge of your little finger positioned close to your right ear.

Step inward and backward with your right foot slowly to adopt the 'fighting stance' (Fig. 21). Bring your left arm gently downwards over your right arm so that your fist traverses diagonally downwards across the front of your body. When you perform this arm action your fist is twisted

39

FIG. 21

to point forward and downward as you imagine that you
are knocking the attacker's right foot aside by contacting
his lower leg with the little-finger edge of your left wrist.
The movement of your left arm is stilled as it becomes
straightened so that your left fist is positioned, palm downwards, some six inches above your left knee (Fig. 22).

Once you have acclimatised yourself to the foregoing
parts of the technique you should also take back your right
fist to your right hip with knuckles toward the ground and
palm uppermost as you institute the blocking action with
your left arm.

While I have segregated the different actions incorporated in the technique, for the sake of clarity, it is important
that the whole compound movement is executed by you as
soon as practical. You should be careful to try out the blocking movement with restraint until you get used to the neces-

FIG. 22

sary twisting action incorporated in the technique. It is a
mistake to use powerful actions at too early a juncture
because of the danger of straining parts of the body which
have not become used to the unusual range of movement.
After a little while you can safely progress to the stage
where you are implementing the technique at speed without loss of technique. When this stage in training is reached
you can gain a vast amount of power in your actions by
using a contrary movement of the arms when you block
with your left and withdraw your right sharply to your
right hip.

Try out the same form of blocking action with your
right arm by substituting left for right when necessary but
remember to start with the slow motion, primary stage at
first (Fig. 23).

FIG. 23

DOWNWARD BLOCK WHEN MOVING

The third stage in progression is to use the blocking action
on the move, as it were. You will need some five yards'
space behind you for accomplishing this. Start by standing
with feet shoulder width apart then form your hands into
fists in the usual manner. Raise your right arm forward
before moving your right leg inward and backwards as you
make a downward block with your left arm and take back
your right fist to your right hip.

Continue by raising your straightened left arm in front
of you then step an extra large pace backwards with your
left foot, by passing your right foot, as you make the blocking action with your right fist and withdraw your left fist
to your left hip. Raise your extended right arm in front of
you until it is parallel to the floor, then take your right leg

42

an extra large pace backward past your left leg and use your left arm to achieve the blocking action.

Clench your hands into fists then straighten your right arm in front of you and move your left fist near to your right ear. In this style of Downward Block you should pivot on the ball of your left foot inwards to your right so that you twist toward your right. When you complete this quarter-turn to your right bend your left leg and step diagonally backwards to your right with your straightened right leg as you make the Downward Block with your left arm.

It is vital throughout your training in Karate that you keep the body as relaxed as possible before making a blocking action or counter attack when you powerfully tense the whole of your body. This dynamic variance from the relaxed state to that of one where your muscles become fully tensed has the aim of gradually increasing the power of your body.

Rising Block

This particular blocking action is effectively employed against any frontal blow aimed at you by the attacker between the lines formed by your shoulders and the top of your head. As usual the essence of the technique is to utilise a twisting action of the whole forearm.

To start your actions quickly adopt the left handed stance of the Downward Block just described by using your left arm with which to block as you withdraw your right fist to your right hip and take back your right leg a large pace.

Now slightly relax your clenched left fist before bending your left arm, as you twist your left fist outward so that the knuckles become twisted downward, when you bring your left forearm diagonally across, and closely to, the front of your body. When the little-finger edge of your left fist nears the front of your right shoulder the direction to which

your left fist and arm moves is suddenly changed. You now
twist your left fist so that the little-finger edge becomes
uppermost as your left forearm moves outwards and
slightly upwards. At the completion of this action your
forearm should be positioned in front of your face at an
angle of 45 degrees to the floor with the knuckles of your

FIG. 24

left fist some twelve inches in front of your forehead
(Fig. 24).

Resume the position of the Downward Block by twisting
your left clenched hand toward yourself as you reverse
your arm movements. Do this by bringing the palm of your
fist to the front of your right shoulder before straightening
your arm as you again twist your left fist so that the palm
of your clenched hand is positioned just above your left
knee (Fig. 25).

It is a very useful exercise to practise the Rising Block
with the Downward Block in the way just described in

order to afford as diverse as possible a twisting action of the lower part of your left arm. After practising the Rising Block many times with your left arm you should adopt the right side version of the Downward Block. Do this by standing with your feet shoulder width apart before moving your

FIG. 25

left foot inward and backward and implement the Downward Block with your right arm as you withdraw your left fist to your left hip. Continue your actions by bringing the palm of your right fist near to the front of your left shoulder before twisting your right fist so that the palm is furthest away from you with your lower arm at an angle of 45 degrees to the surface. You should again practise reverting from the Downward Block to the Rising Block by using your right arm upon this occasion.

It is essential that one of your arms is kept in front of your upper body as otherwise there is a danger of a potential attacker hitting you.

You will need about four yards' pace behind you for practising the Rising Block on the move, as it were.

Take up the left side version of the Downward Block with your left arm used for the blocking action, left leg forward and right fist positioned palm uppermost at your right hip. Start your actions by moving your left fist toward your right shoulder before twisting your left fist outward to assume the position of Rising Block with your left arm.

The next compound action is to take back your left leg in an enlarged pace by-passing your right foot. This means you assume the right leg forward stance when the right leg is bent with the knee turned outwards and the left leg becomes braced behind you. At the same time your right fist is brought outside your left arm as you withdraw your left fist from its blocking position to your left hip and twist your right fist and lower arm into the Rising Block (Fig. 26).

You again move backwards but upon this occasion withdraw your right leg a very large pace as you move your right fist backwards to your right hip when your left fist and lower arm are used to achieve the block.

RISING BLOCK—WHEN MOVING FORWARD

Take up the position of Downward Block with your left arm used for the blocking action and left leg forward. Your right fist should be held by your right hip with the palm uppermost.

Open your left hand as you extend your left arm diagonally upwards until your left hand is in front of your head with the palm of your hand facing to your right. Advance your right leg a large pace forward by moving your right foot inward toward your left foot then outward as you step past your left foot. As your right foot comes to rest

FIG. 26

upon the floor to the side of, and well in front of, your left foot, you perform the Rising Block with your right arm. When you carry out the blocking action with your right arm your left hand is withdrawn, palm uppermost, to your left hip and formed into a fist.

Start to achieve the second blocking movement by opening your right hand as you advance your left leg a very large pace forward. When your left foot touches the floor use your left arm powerfully to make the Rising Block as you speedily close your right hand preparatory to withdrawing your right fist to your right hip.

Begin the third blocking action by unclenching your left hand before upraising your left arm as you advance your right leg forward. Once your right foot is replaced on the floor use your right arm to achieve the Rising Block while sharply withdrawing your left hand, now as a fist, to your left hip.

Inside Block

This type of block is useful in close-quarter fighting. Again it is best to start with the primary stage at first.

Adopt the left side version of the Downward Block so that your bent left leg is in advance of your straightened right leg. Twist your right fist forward, until your arm is parallel to the floor, then bend your left arm and tuck

FIG. 27

your left fist under your right armpit with the knuckles uppermost (Fig. 27). Twist your left fist outwards from under your right armpit to a point some twelve inches in front of your left shoulder. The palm of your hand should be toward you with the arm reasonably well bent and you should imagine that the point of contact with the attackers' arm is on the thumb edge of your left wrist. Concurrently twist your right fist, palm uppermost, as you withdraw it to your right hip. You should keep your left leg bent with

48

your right leg extended behind you and you should have a somewhat wide stance (Fig. 28).

In order to achieve a reasonably flexible arm movement you should not clench your left hand too tightly at the first few attempts. It is also important not to use too much power

FIG. 28

as this technique calls for an awkward twisting action of the arm when you use the block.

INSIDE BLOCK—WHEN MOVING BACKWARDS

You start your actions again by taking up the position of the left side version of the Downward Block. Twist your right fist forward so that your right arm becomes parallel to the floor and bend your left arm as you tuck your left fist, with knuckles uppermost, under your right armpit. Make the Inside Block by utilising your left arm as you

49

withdraw your right fist to your right hip. Continue by straightening your left arm, twisting your fist so that the knuckles become uppermost, as you bend your right arm and tuck your right fist under your left armpit. Take back your left leg in an extra large pace until you can place your left foot on the floor some distance diagonally behind your right foot. As soon as you become firmly balanced flick your right fist outwards from under your left armpit as you withdraw your left fist, palm uppermost, to your left hip.

Continue by straightening your right arm as you twist your fist so that the knuckles of your right fist become uppermost. Tuck your left fist under your right armpit and take an extended pace backward with your right leg. Immediately upon your right foot becoming firmly planted upon the floor flick your left fist outwards as you twist your right fist and withdraw your right fist to your right hip. Ensure that your 'blocking' hand does not go beyond the relative side of your body or above the line formed by your shoulders.

INSIDE BLOCK—WHEN MOVING FORWARD

You are again presumed to be positioned for the left side version of the Downward Block. Step forward with your right foot on the floor close to the inside of your left foot as you straighten your left arm forward and position your right fist close to your left armpit. Follow these actions by stepping forward and outwards with your bent right leg as you implement the Inside Block with your right arm by flicking your right fist outward.

Continue by twisting your right fist as you straighten your right arm forward, tuck your left fist under your right armpit and advance your left foot to the floor close to the inside of your right foot. Progress by stepping forward and outwards with your bent left leg as you flick your left fist outward to execute the inside Block and pull back your right fist to your right hip with the palm uppermost.

Outside Front Block

This type of block is usefully employed for preventing the attacker's head-high blow from reaching you from the side.

Take up the position of the Downward Block with your left side advanced. Straighten your right arm horizontally forward and bend your left arm as you bring your left fist under your right armpit with the palm of your hand uppermost. Now move your left fist outwards and upwards as you twist your left fist so that the palm becomes twisted away from you. Your fist should be positioned about twelve inches away from, and level with, the left side of your head. In order to utilise the power of your body you should hunch your shoulders as you tuck your left fist under your right armpit before expanding your chest as you make the blocking action (Fig. 29).

As usual, you should try the movement in slow motion until you get used to the actions which are called for.

After practising the activity by using your left arm you should switch to using your right arm. For this purpose position yourself in the right side style of the Downward Block with your right leg, side and arm in advance. Twist your left fist as you straighten your left arm forward and bend your right arm to bring your right fist palm uppermost, under your left armpit. Hunch your shoulders before flicking your right wrist outward and upward while twisting your fist so that the palm of your hand faces outward as you expand your chest (Fig. 30).

OUTSIDE FRONT BLOCK—WHEN MOVING BACKWARDS

Resume the position of the left side version of the Downward Block. Straighten your left arm forward as you bring your right fist under your left armpit. Withdraw your left leg an extra pace and accomplish the blocking action with your right arm as your left foot is planted upon the floor and bring your left fist speedily back, palm uppermost, to your left hip.

Straighten your right arm forward and bring your left fist under your right armpit before taking your right leg a large pace backward. Make the outside blocking action with your left arm as you move your right fist back to your

FIG. 29

right hip when your right foot is planted upon the floor diagonally behind your left foot.

Extend your left arm forward as you move your right fist under your left armpit. Take back your left leg in an extended backward step and use your right arm to implement the blocking action as you bring your left fist, palm uppermost, back to your left hip.

FIG. 30

OUTSIDE FRONT BLOCK—WHEN
MOVING FORWARD

Let us assume that you have performed the Downward Block by using your left arm with your left side and leg in advance of your right. Move your left arm forward until it is parallel to the floor and tuck your right fist under your left armpit. Advance your right foot to the floor by the inside of your left foot and without a break in the action step forward and outwards with your right foot. As you replace your right foot firmly on the floor some distance diagonally in front of your left foot use your right arm for the blocking action and withdraw your left fist, palm uppermost, to your left hip.

Straighten your right arm forward as you tuck your left fist under your right armpit. Move your left foot forward close to the inside of your right foot then without pause continue stepping forward with your left foot, placing it on the floor diagonally in front of your right foot. Make the blocking movement by using your left arm as you withdraw your right fist, palm uppermost, to your right hip.

Extend your left arm forward before tucking your right fist under your left armpit. Step forward with your right foot towards the inside of your left foot and then diagonally forward and outward to the floor in front of your left foot. Use your right arm for the blocking action as you withdraw your left fist, with palm uppermost, to your left hip.

Twisting Outside Block (head level)

This type of blocking action is aptly used when the attacker aims a punch at your face from the front.

Commence your actions by executing the left side stance of the Downward Block. Raise your right arm forward until it is parallel to the floor then take back your left shoulder and bend your left arm so that your upraised left fist is uppermost and positioned some twelve inches diagonally behind your left ear. Point the fingers of your right hand forward and ensure that the knuckles of your left fist are nearest to your head with the palm of your left hand facing towards your left side rear (Plate 1).

Implement the block with your left arm by withdrawing your right hand to your right hip as you swing your left bent arm forward and inwards, while twisting your left fist, so that you make the blocking action with your left forearm. As your left forearm comes in front of your face continue twisting your left fist outwards so that the knuckles are outwards with the palm of your left hand situated some twelve inches in front of your forehead. Concurrent with this blocking action your right hand should be formed as a fist and held closely to your right hip in the usual manner.

Now use your right arm with which to block. Adopt the right side stance for the Downward Block. Straighten your left arm forward with fingers pointing to your front as you upraise your right bent arm to your right side and take back your right shoulder. Your right fist should be positioned by the right side of your head with the palm of the hand facing outwards. You now swing your right arm forward and inwards, with the fist uppermost, while twisting your fist inwards until your forearm becomes positioned vertically in front of your head with the right fist uppermost.

Revert from left to right using your left arm and right arm alternately to utilise the blocking action for several minutes.

TWISTING OUTSIDE BLOCK (HEAD LEVEL)—WHEN MOVING BACKWARDS

Take up the left side style of Downward Block. Extend your left arm forward until your arm is parallel to the ground when you extend your fingers to the front. Raise your right arm so that your right fist is brought near to the right side of your head with the palm of your right hand facing outwards. Now take back your left leg, in an exaggerated pace, as you implement the forward blocking action with the lower part of your right arm and withdraw your left hand, in the form of a fist, to your left hip (Fig. 31).

Prepare to execute the blocking action with your left arm by straightening your right arm forward while upraising your left arm with the fist positioned as before. Move your right leg an abnormal pace backwards before using your left arm for the forward blocking action as you simultaneously form your right hand into a fist and take it back to your right hip (Fig. 32).

Carry on by extending your left arm and fingers forward while upraising your right bent arm with the palm of the fist twisted outwards and situated fairly close to your right ear. Take back your left leg and use your right arm to make the blocking action as you withdraw your left fist to your left hip.

FIG. 31

TWISTING OUTSIDE BLOCK (HEAD LEVEL)—WHEN MOVING FORWARD

Let us presume that you adopt the left side method of the Downward Block. Straighten your left arm forward with fingers pointed then raise your right bent arm until your right fist is positioned diagonally behind your right ear with palm outwards. Advance your right foot speedily forward toward the inside of your left foot, then diagonally outwards to the front. When your right foot comes to rest upon the floor diagonally in front of your left foot make the forward blocking action with your right bent arm and withdraw your left hand to your left hip.

Continue by straightening your right arm and fingers forward as you raise your bent left arm upwards so that

56

FIG. 32

your left fist is positioned, in the usual way, slightly behind the left side of your head. Step forward and inward with your left foot towards the inside of your right foot before continuing by then stepping forward and outward with your left foot. Once your left foot is on the floor diagonally in front of your right foot institute the forward blocking action with your left bent arm as you take back your right hand, while clenching it, to your right hip.

Begin to complete your third blocking action by stretching your left arm and fingers forward as you raise your right bent arm with your right fist positioned near to the right side of your head. Advance your right foot quickly towards the inside of your left foot. then outwards until it is diagonally in front of your left foot. As soon as your right foot is replaced upon the floor make the blocking action with your right arm and withdraw your left fist to your left hip.

Twisting Outside Block (chest level)
This form of defence is ideally used to prevent the attacker from punching you in the chest region. It is the same type

FIG. 33

of blocking action as the one just described. The only difference is that the arm which you use to block is positioned lower in the last stage of the movement so that the fist is in front of your chest, level with the line formed by your shoulders. For this reason I do not consider it necessary again to elaborate on all the moves but I urge you not to skim over this blocking action as it will prove a vital part of your general defensive ability (Fig. 33).

58

Knife-edge Block

This blocking action is accomplished with the hand opened in such a way that the little-finger edge of the wrist is brought into contact with the attacker's lower arm. While this form of open-hand block is very useful for nullifying a blow from reaching your chest region it is important to note that there is a certain amount of danger due to the vulnerability of the fingers particularly if one does not keep them pressed closely together.

For the experienced Judoman the blocking action can be usefully brought into play against the attacker.

The hand does not have to be unclenched where a throwing action is used as a counter-attack, as would be the case in most other forms of blocking.

On the other side of the coin, as it were, there is a danger when under attack of hurting your fingers if the attack is made with a foot rather than a hand.

Another major point of difference in the Knife-edge Block, from most other blocking actions, is in the stance. Whereas you have been recommended to adopt a stance where the forward leg is bent in the stance for this present blocking style, the weight is mainly situated on the back leg with the forward leg kept almost straight (a proportion of about sixty per cent to forty per cent).

In order to get used to the technique let's deal with the movement involving the legs before dealing with the actions of your arms.

Let us presume that you are standing upright with your feet about twelve inches apart. Pivot outward on the ball of your right foot until the toes of this foot point directly to your right. Glide your left foot forward some twenty inches so that the toes point directly forward and your left foot is positioned directly in front of your right foot and at right ankles to that foot. You should allow the whole of your left foot to rest upon the floor while your right leg is well bent with the knee turned somewhat inwards. Try out this positioning many times so that you get used to the posture.

Revert to the normal upright stance with your feet some twelve inches apart before twisting your left foot outwards to your left and gliding your right leg forward until your right foot points directly forward in line with, and at right angles to, your left foot. This time your left leg is bent with the knee turned partially inwards. Once again you should perform this movement many times in slow motion.

After you have gained some general idea of the actions called for by your legs you are able to incorporate the arm and body movements to execute the compound action.

Let us start again with the left foot version of this blocking action. Keeping your fingers pressed closely together, extend your straightened right arm forward in front of you, with palm downward, so that your right arm is parallel to the floor. Bend your left arm and bring your left hand over your right arm to a position close to your right ear with the palm of your hand situated nearest to your ear and fingers pointed backwards to the direction over your right shoulder.

Advance your left leg forward as you twist your right foot outward with toes directly pointed to your right as you bend your right leg and adopt the 'back stance'. Simultaneously with this leg action flick your left hand forward and slightly outward until your left hand is positioned some fifteen to eighteen inches in front of your left shoulder with the arm kept slightly bent. The little finger edge of your hand is furthest away and the thumb nearest you. To gain maximum power in the blocking action the right hand is also withdrawn by twisting your thumb outwards until the edge of your little finger contacts the middle of your chest with the fingers pointed towards the imaginary attacker (Fig. 34).

Once you have made the blocking action move your arms back to their original position with your straight right arm held horizontally in front of you and your left arm bent with the palm of your left hand situated close to your right ear. Continue these arm actions for several minutes so that you implement many blocking movements in slow motion with the outside edge of your left wrist and hand while still maintaining the back stance.

Now try the blocking action out by using your right arm. Start by positioning your left arm horizontally in front of you with the palm of your right hand poised near

FIG. 34

to your left ear. Advance your right foot directly in front of your left foot as you pivot outwards on your left foot until it is printed directly to your left and bend your left leg.

Achieve the blocking action by using your right lower arm as you withdraw your left arm (Fig. 35).

Try the movements out many times in slow motion before continuing.

FIG. 35

KNIFE-EDGE BLOCK—WHEN MOVING BACKWARDS

Stand upright with your feet about twelve inches apart. Extend your right arm horizontally forward and bring your left hand upwards over your right arm with the palm of your left hand near to your right ear. Do not move your left leg but step backwards with your right leg and point your right foot directly outwards to your right as you re-place your right foot upon the floor about twenty inches directly behind your left foot. Bend your right leg, turning your right knee slightly inwards as you allow your left leg to become almost straightened. Implement the blocking action in the way previously described by flicking your left hand forward and outward as you twist your right

62

hand outward before withdrawing your right hand to the middle of your chest.

It is important that you consciously prevent your shoulders from becoming even slightly raised but instead concentrate on keeping your back straight with shoulders set.

After accomplishing the blocking action with your left arm straighten this arm horizontally forward with palm of the hand downwards and move the palm of your right hand over your left arm to near your left ear.

Take back your left leg, in an extended pace, until it is some twenty inches behind your right foot and replace your left foot upon the floor with toes pointed directly to your left as you swivel your right foot inwards so that it comes to point directly forward. Bend your left leg as you lower your left knee slightly inwards and allow your right leg to become almost straightened in front of you. Bring about the blocking action by flicking your right hand forward and outward as you twist your left hand before withdrawing this hand to the middle of your chest so that the little finger contacts your chest.

Now begin to implement the third blocking action. Straighten your right arm horizontally forward with palm facing the floor as you move your left hand above your right arm near to your left ear. Take back your right leg and replace your right foot upon the floor with the toes pointed directly to your right as you twist your left foot until it points directly forward in front of you. Bend your right leg as you allow your left leg to become straightened. Make the blocking action with your left lower arm as you withdraw your right hand to your chest.

KNIFE-EDGE BLOCK—WHEN MOVING FORWARD

When you advance a leg to perform the Knife-edge Block it is the opposite to normal walking in that the weight of your body is kept mainly situated on the back leg instead of being swayed forward on to the forward leg.

Stand with your feet about twelve inches apart then straighten your right arm horizontally forward in front of you and bring your left hand over your right arm until the palm of your left hand is close to your right ear. Advance your left foot forward some fifteen or twenty inches in front of your right foot as you twist your right foot outwards until it points directly to your right when you bend your right leg. As you adopt the 'back stance' make the blocking action with the lower part of your left arm as you withdraw your right hand to the middle of your chest.

Carry on by straightening your left arm forward as you bring your right hand over your left arm so that the palm of your right hand is near to your left ear. Advance your right leg in an extra large pace to in front of your left foot as you twist your left foot until it points directly outward to your left when you bend your left leg. Use your right arm to achieve the blocking action by flicking your right hand forward and outwards as you withdraw your left hand to the middle of your chest.

Extend your right hand and arm forward before bringing your left hand over your right arm to a point near to your right ear. Make an extra large pace with your left foot to the floor in front of your right foot as you twist your right foot outwards and bend your right leg. Perform the third blocking technique with the lower part of your left arm as you withdraw your right hand to your chest.

Once you have practised the blocking movement many times switch from retreating to advancing, while utilising the blocking action with the lower part of your left and right lower arms.

Inward-twisting Block

This blocking action is aptly used at close-quarters if the attacker attempts to smash his fist or elbow against your ribs. Quite apart from this first consideration a secondary benefit derived by using this blocking action is the confidence in your ability which it promotes by getting used to stopping blows at close range.

Take up the left side method of the Downward Block with your left arm and left leg forward. Move your left fist to your left hip with palm uppermost as you stretch your right arm partially forward. Move your left fist diagonally forward as you twist your left fist so that the knuckles of your left hand face toward you and your left elbow is brought inwards so that it is in front of your chest. Your forearm is now parallel to your upper body with the fist pointed towards the ground. You should imagine that you are contacting the attacker's arm with the little-finger edge of your left wrist. As you implement this blocking action you should withdraw your right hand to your right hip in the form of a fist as you twist your hips to your right to add power to your blocking action (Fig. 36).

FIG. 36

Now try the blocking action by using your right arm. Take up the right side position of the Downward Block with your right leg and arm in advance. Partially straighten your left arm forward and move your right fist back to your right hip with palm uppermost. Now move your right foot diagonally forward as you twist your right hand so that your knuckles are nearest to you and your right elbow is brought inwards in front of your chest. Your right forearm is parallel to your upper body with fist pointed downward. As you accomplish this blocking action with your right arm withdraw your left hand in the form of a fist to your left hip, and twist your hips slightly to your left to add power to your movements.

INWARD-TWISTING BLOCK—WHEN MOVING BACKWARDS

Adopt the left side version of the Downward Block with your left side, leg and arm in advance of your right. Your right fist should be well placed by your right hip and you should partially straighten your left forearm forward. Withdraw your left leg in an exaggerated pace backwards past the inside of your right foot and implement the blocking action with the lower part of your right arm and fist in the way described earlier. Your right lower arm should be parallel to your body with your right fist pointed downward and your knuckles twisted toward you. You gain additional power in the blocking movement by twisting your hips to the left as you take back your left fist to your left hip (Fig. 37).

Continue by removing your right leg a large pace backwards past your left foot. Implement the blocking action with your left forearm and fist as you twist your hips to the right and withdraw your right fist to your right hip.

Now shift your left leg a large pace backwards as you make the blocking action with your right forearm and fist. At the same time move your left fist back to your left hip and twist your hips to your left.

FIG. 37

INWARD-TWISTING BLOCK—WHEN MOVING FORWARD

You are taken to be in the position of left side style for the Downward Block with your left clenched hand reasonably near to your left knee and right fist at your right hip.

Step forward with your right leg, in an extra large pace past your left foot. As your right leg is advanced prepare to move your right fist diagonally inwards before twisting your right hand in order that your knuckles are toward you with your right forearm parallel to your upper body. Concurrently move your left fist back to your left hip, palm uppermost, as you slightly advance your right shoulder and twist your hips to your left.

Continue by implementing the next blocking action with your left forearm. Take an extended pace forward with your left leg past your right leg. Twist your left arm inwards to achieve the blocking action with your left forearm as you withdraw your right fist to your right hip. Advance your left shoulder as you twist your hips slightly to your right in order to impart power into the blocking action of your left arm.

Now advance your right leg past your left leg before implementing the blocking action with your right arm as you withdraw your left fist to your left hip and twist your hips to your left.

Cross-armed Block

The Cross-armed Block is a most useful and powerful blocking action which can be aptly utilised against either a downward blow to your head or a kick to your stomach region.

Adopt the position of the left side method of the Downward Block. Move your clenched fists toward one another and cross your arms at the wrists, with the right wrist uppermost, just in front of the left side of your stomach. Now thrust your fists rather diagonally upwards at speed until your clenched fists are above and in front of your head. As you make this lunging action with your arms and shoulders tense your stomach muscles in order to gain as much power as possible in the upward blocking action (Plate 2).

Try out the upward blocking action many times.

Now accomplish the following downward blocking action. Stand with feet about shoulder width apart then move your clenched fists to the position above the front of your right shoulder with the thumb of your right hand nearest your right shoulder (Fig. 38). Move your bent left leg forward as you make a powerful downward blocking action with your forearms by thrusting your clenched fists downwards, with right over left, to a point just in front of your stomach. Your stomach muscles should be tensed as this action takes effect (Fig. 39).

FIG. 38

As usual try the blocking action many times in slow motion to gain some knowledge of the movements involved.

CROSS-ARMED BLOCK—WHEN MOVING
BACKWARDS

Let us presuppose that you are in the position of the left side posture for Downward Block.

Move your fists near to the left side of your stomach and cross your arms at the wrists with your right wrist uppermost. Take back your left leg in an exceptional pace and then straighten your crossed arms powerfully upward and forward to implement the blocking action. Continue retreating by beginning to move your right leg in a large

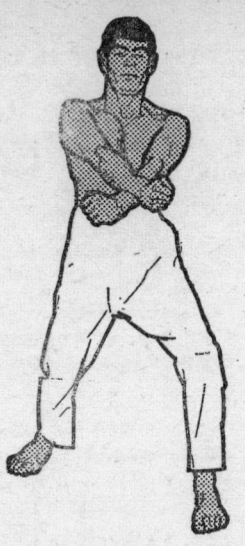

FIG. 39

backward step. Upraise your fists above your right shoulder and your arms crossed at the wrists. As soon as your right foot becomes planted upon the floor institute the blocking action. Do this by powerfully straightening your arms diagonally downwards until your fists are positioned in front of your stomach with the right fist uppermost and knuckles inside.

CROSS-ARMED BLOCK—WHEN MOVING FORWARD

Let us take it for granted that you are in the usual position of the left side Downward Block. Move your fists near to the left side of your abdomen before crossing your arms at the wrists with your right wrist uppermost. Advance your right leg in a large pace and immediately that you replace your right foot upon the floor powerfully straighten your crossed arms forward and diagonally upward to a point in front of your head. Continue by bending your crossed arms so that your fists are brought close to the front of your right shoulder with your right fist nearest your shoulder. Advance your left leg in a large pace and as soon as your left foot is replaced firmly upon the floor thrust your clenched fists downward to a point just in front of your stomach to make the downward blocking action with your crossed arms.

Double-handed Knife-edge Block

This form of blocking action is used when the attacker attempts to swing the whole of his arm against your upper body or face. The aim of such an attacker, who is facing the same direction as you while standing side by side with you, could be to swing his straightened arm forward and then powerfully backwards to knock you over backwards. Alternately the attacker could be facing you before stepping to your side and swinging his straightened right arm forward against your upper body to knock you over backwards.

You should stand upright with your feet about shoulder width apart and arms at your sides. Keep your hands un-clenched with fingers extended and pressed closely together. Suddenly bend your arms so that your hands are brought near to your right shoulder then flick your lower arms forward so that your hands are some twelve inches in front of your chest with palms facing inwards and some ten or twelve inches away from each other (Fig. 40). Just you execute this arm action tense your stomach muscles and move your left leg a trifle forward while inclinging your upper body forward.

Your aim in training should be to practise the actions until you can make a sudden and powerful blocking action.

Blocking an attack with the knee

It is not always practical to use your arm to knock aside a blow when the attacker uses his knee, particularly if he is very close to you.

It is unwise to stand squarely facing a potential attacker but looking on the black side of things, this like any other precept of self-defence cannot always be adhered to under diverse circumstances. The main factor to bear in mind, even if you are caught totally unprepared, is that you must twist your hips sharply to one direction while lowering a knee inwards. This means that your lower body will become turned partially sideways and the attacker is thus foiled in

FIG. 40

his aim of smashing his knee into your stomach or groin. While this manœuvre will entail the attacker's knee catching you on the thigh it is prefereable to sustaining hurt to more vulnerable parts of your body.

The best defence against the attacker who attempts force-fully to bring his knee into contact with your stomach re-gion is to counter him in turn by using your knee as a wea-pon against the thigh of his leg. You can achieve this by bringing your knee forward and inwards so that your knee is forcefully driven into the inside of his corresponding thigh.

You can practise for this contingency by using your left knee and right knee alternately to make a diagonally forward blow as though you intend to strike the attacker's thigh a severe blow.

You should move about the room, or wherever you hap-

FIG. 41

pen to be practising, until you can smoothly implement the actions which are called for (Fig. 41).

Blocking 'low-level' Kick

If the attacker aims a kick at your shin, or even knee, it is not generally efficient to attempt knocking his leg aside with a forearm blocking action. In this event you would have to use the sole of your foot or shoe against his instep or ankle so that he literally disables himself by forcefully bringing his lower leg or foot into contact with the sole or edge of your shoe.

Let us imagine for our purposes that the attacker will

FIG. 42

lash out with his right foot at your left shin. Twist to your left and step well away from him on to your left leg which should be kept bent. Raise your right leg from the floor before turning your right foot inwards and position your foot in line with his supposed oncoming ankle (Fig. 42).

As usual practise both by using your left foot and right foot while moving about the room.

Combination Blocking Technique

Due to the fact that the attacker may violently assault you with a series of blows it is imperative to prepare yourself for the second stage of defence, as it were, by linking the blocking actions together. After you have accomplished the following compound blocking actions which I recommend for training purposes, you should dart about the practice area and use any number of blocking actions so that you become well versed in varying your forms of defence.

Inside Block, Rising Block and Downward Block

The basis of this threefold blocking action when moving forward is to implement the Inside Block as you step forward with your left leg, followed by the Rising Block as you advance your right leg and then the Downward Block as you again move your left leg forward.

Stand upright with your feet placed closely together and clenched hands positioned by the respective sides of your body.

Raise your straightened right arm in front of you until it is parallel to the ground and then tuck your left fist under your right armpit. Step outward and forwards with your left bent leg and implement the Inside Block by flicking your bent left arm outwards until your left fist is stilled just as it is in line with and in front of your left shoulder. Concurrently sharply withdraw your right fist to your right hip (Fig. 43).

Now prepare to utilise the Rising Block. Straighten your left arm upwards in front of and above your head as you advance your right foot inwards to your left foot then forward and outwards. Just as you replace your right foot upon the floor make the Rising Block with your slightly bent right arm. Do this by bringing your right fist diagonally forward before twisting your fist inward as you flick your right arm upwards and powerfully withdraw your left

FIG. 43

fist to your left hip (Fig. 44). You are now in a position to
utilise the Downward Block. Lower your right arm somewhat as you straighten it when it becomes horizontally
positioned, fist forward, in front of you. Bend your left
arm as you bring your left fist over your right upper arm
so that the palm of your hand is close to your right ear.
Continue by stepping a large pace forward and outwards
with your left bent leg and accomplish a strong Downward
Block. Achieve this with your left arm by flicking your left
fist downwards and outwards to a point just above your
left knee as you move your right fist back to your right hip.

Now try the same three blocking actions from your last
position of the left side version of the Downward Block
while moving backwards.

Raise your left arm forward until it is parallel to the
floor and then tuck your right fist under your left armpit.

You are now in position to perform Inside Block. Step a large pace backwards with your left leg as you flick your bent right arm outward and sharply move your left fist back to your left hip.

Execute the Rising Block with your left bent arm by moving your left fist diagonally forward and then upwards as you withdraw your right fist to your right hip and take your right leg to your rear.

Finalise your actions by using your right arm to make the Downward Block. Lower your left arm slightly while straightening it when it is horizontally in front of you when you bring your right fist over your upper left arm near to your left ear. Move your left leg in a large pace backwards and then flick your right arm downwards to perform the Downward Block when your right fist is stilled in motion

FIG. 44

just above your right knee and your left fist is quickly pulled back to your left hip.

It is well worth while to practise moving forward and backward over and over again to get used to linking the blocking actions.

Outside Front Block, Downward Block and Rising Block

In this form of training the aim is to rely on one arm to accomplish three blocking actions rather than to use each arm alternately. At first, let's consider the moves while moving forward.

Adopt the left side version of the Downward Block with your left side in advance of your right and right fist at your right hip. Raise your straight left arm in front of yourself until it is parallel to the surface and tuck your right fist under your left armpit. Now step forward and outwards with your right foot as you flick your right fist outwards and upwards. You should still your actions when your right fist is positioned with knuckles nearest you some twelve inches away from the right side of your head. Now use your right arm to perform the Downward Block. Achieve this by speedily moving your right fist laterally and then downwards to the point above your right knee (Fig. 45).

Continue by using the Rising Block with your right arm. Move your right fist quickly back towards your right hip before twisting it and flicking your right forearm upwards into the position of Rising Block.

You now use your left arm to make the three blocking actions. Straighten your right arm forward as you tuck your left fist under your right armpit. Step forward and outwards onto your left bent leg as you jerk your left fist outwards and upwards to bring the Outside Front Block into play. Carry on your moves by moving your left fist across your body and over your right arm to the point close to your right ear. Speedily jerk your left fist downwards to perform the Downward Block with your left arm. Execute the Rising Block by moving your left fist quickly back to

78

your left hip before twisting it and thrusting it forward into the Rising Block.

You are now in a position to complete the third set of three blocking actions. Straighten your left arm, with fist pointed forward, and tuck your right fist under your left armpit. Step forward and outwards on to your right bent leg

FIG. 45

as you jerk your right fist outwards and upwards to make the Outside Front Block. Move your right fist quickly across your body and left arm to your left ear before flicking your right arm downwards into Downward Block. Withdraw your right fist to your right hip before shooting it forward and then upwards into Rising Block.

You should now try the three sets of blocking actions while retreating. We will assume that you have just completed the Rising Block with your right arm with right bent leg in advance. Straighten your right arm forward and tuck your left fist under your right armpit. Move your right leg backwards in a large pace as you jerk your left fist outwards and upwards to perform Outside Front Block. Continue by moving your left fist back across your body to near your right ear before utilising your left arm powerfully to accomplish the Downward Block. Complete the set of moves by moving your left fist towards your left hip before flicking your fist forward and upward to make Rising Block.

Stretch your left arm forward then tuck your right fist under your left armpit. Move your left leg in a large pace backwards as you twist your right fist outwards and upwards into the position of Outside Front Block. Progress by passing your right fist across the front of your body to your left ear prior to executing Downward Block with your right arm. Move your right fist back to your right hip while twisting your fist, before swinging your right arm forward and upwards into Rising Block.

Extend your right arm forward before tucking your left fist under your right armpit. Move your right leg in a large pace backwards as you twist your left fist outwards and upwards into the Outside Front Block. Bring your left fist across the front of your body to your right ear before implementing Downward Block so that your left fist is brought above your left knee. Move your left fist back to your left hip while twisting your fist before swinging your left arm forward and upwards into Rising Block.

At first you will find that the inactive arm is somewhat of an hindrance to your quick blocking actions. In reality this arm would be used for counter-attacking, or indeed additional blocking, and it is thus a good idea to move it forward and back to its respective hip in contradiction to the other arm. When you become well versed in the other actions this means that when one hand is forward in a blocking action the other is positioned at the hip and when the hand being used to block is moved back in between blocks the other hand is moved forward.

Quite apart from the arm actions this compound blocking action will call for a change of stance from that of the so-called back stance to that of the forward stance.

Stand upright with your feet about shoulder width apart with your hands positioned by your sides. Swing your right arm forward so that the palm is downward when the arm becomes parallel to the floor. Move your left hand to a point near to your right ear with the palm of your left hand nearest your right ear. Pivot outwards on the ball of your right foot until the toes of your right foot point directly to your right when you well bend your right leg. Glide your almost straight left leg diagonally forward and replace your foot on the floor some eighteen inches directly in front of your right foot. Once your left foot is replaced firmly upon the floor you should make the Knife-edge Block with your left lower arm and hand. Do this by twisting your left hand outwards and slightly downwards to the point in front of your left shoulder. Simultaneously twist your right hand and withdraw it to the middle of your chest so that the little finger edge of your hand presses against your breast-bone (Fig. 46).

Move your right hand and form it into a fist with palm uppermost. Step well forward on to your bent right leg as you begin to move your right fist diagonally forward. Bring your right elbow inwards before twisting your right fist so that the knuckles of your right hand are turned toward yourself and your right forearm is parallel to your upper body with your right fist pointed toward the ground. Concurrently form your left hand into a fist and withdraw it swiftly to your left hip. This completes the movement for the Inward-twisting Block.

Straighten your right arm forward with knuckles of your right fist uppermost. Take back your left shoulder and bend your left arm so that your upraised left fist is uppermost and situated about twelve inches diagonally behind your left ear. The knuckles of your left fist should be the nearest part of your hand to your head. Step forward on to your bent left leg and implement the blocking action by swinging your left arm forward and slightly downwards as you twist your left fist so that the knuckles are furthest away from you and your fist is in front of your left shoul-

FIG. 46

der. As you accomplish the Twisting Outside Block withdraw your right fist to your right hip.

Once you have completed the three blocking actions while moving forward try them out when moving backwards.

You have performed the first three advancing blocking actions ending with Twisting Outside Block with your left arm.

Straighten your left arm horizontally forward with your

FIG. 47

hand unclenched and palm downwards. Bring your open
right hand over your left arm to near your left ear with
the palm of your hand nearest to your ear. Take back your
left bent leg in an exaggerated pace so that your left foot
points directly to your left and your right leg becomes
straight as you adopt the back stance with feet in line. Your
right hand should be flicked outwards and slightly downwards until it is positioned in front of your right shoulder.
At the same time you achieve a contrary arm action by
withdrawing your unclenched left hand to the middle of
your chest so that the little finger of your left hand presses
against your breast bone.

After you have made Knife-edge Block with your right
hand you will be ready to make Inward-twisting Block.
Form your left hand into a fist and move it back beyond
your left hip with palm uppermost. Take back your right
leg, in an extended pace, while bending it as you start to

bring your left fist diagonally forward. As soon as your right foot is replaced upon the floor quickly move your left elbow inwards before twisting your left fist in order that your forearm is parallel to your upper body with your left fist pointed towards the floor. This completes Inward-twisting Block.

Extend your left arm horizontally forward with palm of your left hand downwards. Withdraw your right shoulder and bend your right arm so that you hold your right fist aloft, with palm outwards, diagonally behind your right ear. Withdraw your left leg in an exaggerated pace while swinging your right arm inwards and slightly downwards as you twist your right fist to turn the knuckles away from you. You should still the action of your lower right arm when your right fist comes in front of your right shoulder and withdraw your left fist to your left hip (Fig. 47).

The Technique of Counter-attack

Before you consider the technique of counter-attack it is necessary to learn the Karate method of delivering a blow after you have utilised one or more of the blocking actions described earlier.

There are hundreds of different methods of utilising parts of your body for delivering a blow in Karate. For our present purpose I think it best that we concentrate on effectiveness coupled with ease of learning and place these two considerations above all others. This means that you do not jeopardise your possible future safety by attempting to learn too many different facets of defence against a particular attack but bear in mind the adage—maximum effect with minimum effort.

The way to punch—to the chest region
When delivering a counter punch the method is to apply a twisting action of the lower part of the arm being used

in order to impart power to your action in the same way as you gained power for the blocking actions we considered earlier. From the outset you must be careful to see that you use the power of your whole body to increase the power of your counter punches rather than merely using your arm and shoulder muscles.

Adopt the left side style of the Downward Block with

FIG. 48

your right unclenched hand positioned by your right hip then unclench your left hand and straighten your left arm directly forward so that it is parallel to the floor with palm downwards. Make sure that your back is perfectly straight with your weight firmly planted upon the floor. On no account should you be lightly poised on the soles of your feet but instead keep a flat-footed stance (Fig. 48).

Now very slowly move your right fist directly forward, with palm uppermost some twelve inches while literally sliding the little-finger edge of your right wrist and forearm against your right side. When your right elbow is positioned at your right hip continue slowly moving your right fist forward (Fig. 49). As the movement of your right arm continues, twist your left hand outwards while forming it into a fist and start to withdraw it to your left hip.

FIG. 49

When your right arm becomes almost extended horizontally in front of you twist your right fist inwards so that your knuckles become uppermost. At the same instant advance your right hip and tense your whole body while pulling back your left hand to your left hip. Ensure that when you make the punching action your knuckles are in line with your wrist in a straight line and imagine that you are punching the attacker in the chest while squarely facing him (Fig. 50).

You should make many slow and gentle punching actions,

concentrating on gaining the required technique. This means giving prime importance to twisting the fist at the last moment, twisting the hips and tensing the whole body as you make the punch.

After gaining a good working knowledge of punching in slow motion you should make progress by making quicker

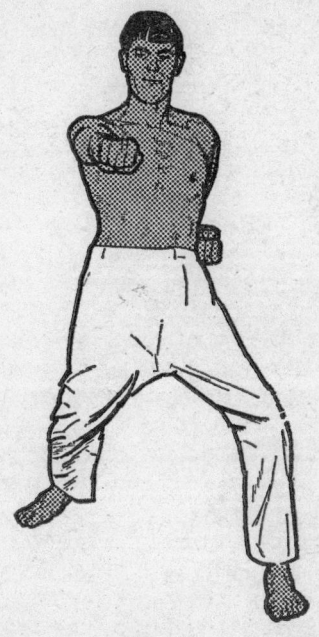

FIG. 50

and stronger punching actions. It is a mistake solely to focus your thoughts on the forward movement of your right arm. The contrary movement of your left fist being withdrawn at speed in order to gain the power of your hips being slightly but swiftly twisted is equally important.

Without changing your stance you should practise using your left hand with which to punch but remember to start with the primary stage by making slow-motion movements.

Stepping Punch—to the chest region

After you have acquired a good basic knowledge of performing the punching action from the static stance you are ready to make the Stepping Punch. I have carefully studied the manner in which Japanese Champions effect the punching action and it appears that they place great emphasis on thrusting their hips and stomachs forward as they dart forward and quickly 'anchor' their feet upon the ground just as the punch is being delivered.

Take up the stance of the left side version of the Downward Block and prepare to make three stepping punches to your front.

Extend your left arm horizontally forward and then step slowly forward and slightly outwards on to your right bent leg. Make your punching action by moving your right fist directly forward before twisting it at the last moment so that the knuckles become uppermost as your left fist is moved back to your left hip. Continue by keeping your right fist momentarily in front of you as you step forward and implement a slow punching action with your left fist. Once your left arm becomes reasonably extended withdraw your right fist to your right hip.

Complete the three-step movement by punching forward with your left fist as you withdraw your right fist to your right hip.

There are two main errors to guard against when using the stepping punch. If the wrist and forearm of the arm with which you are punching with are not kept close to the relevant side of your body for as long as practicable the punch is not straight and powerful. Also if your head and upper body are inclined forward your power is diminished. As I observed earlier the hips must be pushed forward with your back kept straight and head upright.

Once you have completed the last punching action with your left fist bring it to your left ear and then turn completely about to your left by withdrawing your left side and left leg before making the Downward Block with your left arm. You should now be facing the opposite direction to which you were originally facing. Straighten your left arm forward before stepping forward on to your right bent leg. Make the punching action with your right arm as you move your left fist back to your left hip. Carry on your moves by stepping forward with your left leg, punching with your left fist and withdrawing your right fist to your right hip. Finalise the three punching actions to this direction by using your right fist to punch with as you step forward upon your right bent leg and withdraw your left fist to your left hip.

Now try the three-step punching action while retreating step by step.

Let's presume you are in the last position just outlined with your right fist and right bent leg forward. Withdraw your right leg in a large pace as you punch forward with your left fist. Your left leg should be bent as you move your right fist back to your right hip. Progress by withdrawing your left leg while bending your right leg. You then punch forward with your right fist as you withdraw your left fist to your left hip. Finish your movements by moving your right leg back as you bend your left leg and effect the punching action with your left fist.

You should practise moving alternately forward and backward while using the punching actions until you get used to the required movements.

Stepping Punch—to nose
The only main difference between using this form of punch and the one just described is in the angle of the arm which you use for punching. In this method your arm is positioned at an angle of about 30 degrees in relation to the surface instead of horizontally when you complete the punching action (Fig. 51).

On no account should you stand upright and deliver a horizontal blow but ensure that your feet are well planted upon the floor with your forward leg bent.

Your fist is moved forward and upward and twisted at the last moment so that the knuckles become uppermost

FIG. 51

when the arm becomes fully extended at the recommended angle of 30 degrees with the floor.

Try out the punching action from the Downward Block stance at first then when moving forward and backward as you did when punching to the imaginary attacker's chest.

Combination counter-punches

In this method of counter attack you make three consecutive punching actions—one to nose and two to chest level.

Take up the position of the left side Downward Block so that your left bent leg and arm are in advance. Raise your left arm horizontally forward before making a punching action with your right fist to the imaginary attacker's nose. Your right fist should be twisted just as your right arm becomes extended at an angle of about 30 degrees in relation to the floor. When you make this punching action your left fist should be quickly moved back to your left hip (Fig. 52). Continue by punching forward with your left fist at chest level while withdrawing your right fist and then finalise the three punching actions by punching forward with your right fist at chest level and withdraw your left fist to your left hip (Fig. 53).

When you have finished the compound movement leave your right fist forward momentarily as you begin to make a head-high punch with your left fist and then retract your right fist to your right hip. Perform the double punching action at chest level first with your right fist as you withdraw your left fist, then with your left as you withdraw your right fist.

Now try out this batch of punching actions in sets of three, while advancing. Again let's take it that you are in the position of Downward Block with left leg and arm in advance. Raise your left arm until it is horizontal to the

FIG. 52

floor then move your right foot forward near to the surface
by the inside of your left foot before continuing by moving
it forward and outwards and planting it on the floor diagonally in front of your left foot. Immediately make a head-
high angled punch with your right fist as you retract your
left fist to your left hip in the accepted way. Perform two

FIG. 53

quick level punching actions starting with your left fist as
you move your right fist back, then accomplish the punching action with your right fist as you take back your left fist.
Leave your right fist forward momentarily as you move
your left foot forward near to the inside of your right foot
before stepping forward and outward, without pause, so
that you plant your left foot upon the floor diagonally in
front of your right foot. As soon as your left foot is securely
placed upon the floor make the angled head-high punch
with your left fist while moving your right fist back to

your right hip. Make the last of the set of punches with your left fist as you retract your right fist to your right hip.

For the last set of three punching actions move your right foot near to your left foot and then forward and out-wards before planting your right foot on the floor diagon-ally in front of your left foot. Implement the head-high angled punching action with your right fist as you retract your left fist. Speedily punch forward with your left fist and withdraw your right fist to your right hip. Finalise this set of punches by making an horizontal forward punch with your right fist as you move your left fist back to your left hip.

Now let's consider the three groups of punches while you are retreating. Let us presume that you have performed the last punching action just described when your right fist and right leg are forward.

Withdraw your right leg in an extended backward pace and replace your right foot firmly upon the floor obliquely behind your left foot. Use your left fist to punch forward at head level as you move your right fist back to your left hip. Make a straight punch with your right hand as you move your left fist back to your left hip. Quickly reverse your arm actions by punching forward with your left fist as you withdraw your right fist to your right hip.

Take back your left leg in an extra large step and replace your left foot upon the surface obliquely behind your right foot. Utilise your right fist to make a head-high punch as you retract your left fist to your left hip. Punch forward with your left fist and withdraw your right fist then speedily reverse your arm actions by punching forward with your right fist then move your left fist back to your left hip.

Move your right leg in an inordinate backward pace before using your left fist to deliver a head-high blow as you return your right fist to your right hip. Make a forward-punching action with your right fist while withdrawing your left fist then revert by punching forward with your left fist while bringing your right fist back to your right hip. This completes the moves.

I recommend you to try out these combined punching actions by moving forward and backward many times. The three essentials are that you attain a firmly balanced stance directly you complete your stepping movements, keep the leg which is forward bent, and keep your back straight throughout.

Blows with elbow

When the attacker is at close quarters your elbow can be utilised to strike a powerful retaliatory blow to his chin or to the region of his chest.

There are four general ways of delivering a blow with your elbow. Let us consider each individual method.

Upward blow with elbow

This method of striking with the elbow is meant to deliver a blow to the attacker's chin when he is very close to you.

Stand in the position of Downward Block with your left leg and arm forward. Your right fist is positioned by your right hip in the usual way. Now step forward upon your right bent leg and move your right fist upward to the top of your right shoulder close to the right side of your neck. As you make this arm movement your arm becomes fully bent and the palm of your right fist should be nearest the right side of your neck (Fig. 54).

You will probably find this essential arm movement somewhat awkward at the beginning due to the unusual range of movement called for by your right arm but this apparent clumsiness is soon overcome. The main point to remember is to think of striking with the right elbow while tensing your stomach muscles for additional power.

Forward blow with elbow

For the purpose of describing this specific way of striking the attacker's ribs with your left elbow we will presume that you are posed with your right bent leg in advance of your left in the right side version of Downward Block. Your left fist is poised close to your left hip in the accepted

94

manner. Step forward upon your bent left leg before twisting your shoulders as you swing your left elbow forward and inward. Once your arm is parallel to the floor twist your fist to ensure that the knuckles of your left hand are uppermost with your fist almost touching your breast-bone. At the same time retract your right fist to your right hip (Fig. 55).

FIG. 54

Power is added to your elbow by the purposeful twisting action of your shoulders and contrary movement of your right fist being sharply withdrawn to your right hip.

Sideways blow with elbow

This form of elbow jab is made horizontally when you are sideways to the attacker. We will assume that you administer the blow with your right elbow.

You are taken to be in the right side stance of the Down-ward Block with your right leg and right arm in advance. Move your right foot directly to your left until it is directly in front of your left foot and some twenty or so inches away from this foot. Pivot partially outwards on the ball of your left foot as you twist your body to your left so that your

FIG. 55

body is turned directly to this direction. The toes of your feet should be turned slightly inwards as you well bend your legs before twisting your knees outward in the stance of KIBA DACHI.

Fold your arms loosely across the front of your body so that they are parallel to the floor with your right arm above your left arm. Your fists should be positioned close to their opposite shoulders with knuckles uppermost. Look towards your right over your right shoulder so that you look toward the imagined attacker. Now jab your right elbow directly

96

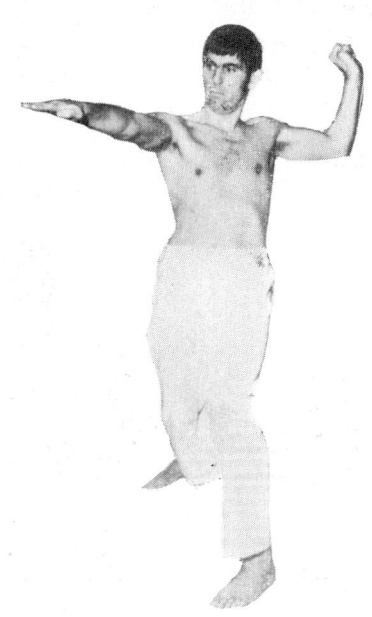

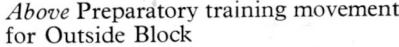

Above Preparatory training movement
for Outside Block

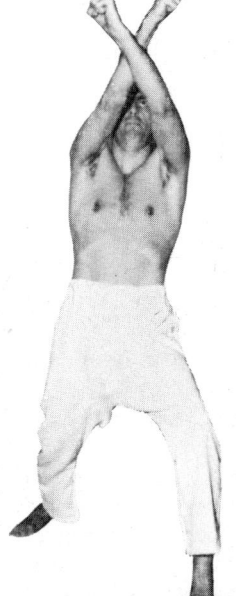

Left 'Cross-armed' Block

Side Kick

Back Kick

'Roundhouse' Kick

Backward blow with fist

Outside Block (shoulder level)

'Reverse' Punch to chest

forward to your right and still the blow when the thumb of your right fist is near to your right nipple. At the same time sharply retract your left fist to your left hip while tensing your whole body (Fig. 56).

The stance of Kiba Dachi is a very strong, well-balanced posture, which may be usefully brought into play when using a sideways or backward blow with the elbow against

FIG. 56

the attacker. The position of the legs is similar to that adopted for horse-back riding. Indeed it is probable that this stance was originally devised for fighting when astride a horse.

Backward blow with elbow

This particular way of striking with the elbow in a backward blow is very useful as a defence if you are attacked from, or held from, behind.

Stand with your feet spaced about shoulder-width apart

with legs bent. Clench your hands to form fists then loosely
fold them in front of your chest so that your bent arms are
parallel to the floor with knuckles of your fists uppermost
and right arm above left arm. Twist your hips and upper
body sharply to your right and make a sharp backwards
blow with your right elbow as you look to your rear and

FIG. 57

tense your stomach muscles. Retract your left fist to your
left hip (Fig. 57). Once you have made a backward blow
with your right elbow revert to your starting position before making a backward blow with your left elbow. Rem-
ber to twist your hips and upper body to your left as you
tense your stomach muscles.

You should also utilise an angled blow with each elbow
by practising jabbing your elbow backwards at an angle
of about 45 degrees so that you could administer a sharp
blow to the attacker's chin.

Added power can sometimes be advantageously utilised behind the power of your elbow blow by cupping the fist within the palm of your other hand. You then drive your elbow backwards.

Combination blows with elbows

Once you have gained some practical knowledge of using your elbows as a counter-attack weapon, with the four basic methods just outlined, it is well worth while to combine them. This will enable you to gain the required fluidity in movement while incorporating the power of your body.

ADVANCING

Start by adopting the left side pose of Downward Block. Step forward on to your right bent leg as you thrust your right elbow upwards while fully bending your right arm so that the palm of your right fist is near to the right side of your neck. Simultaneously move your left fist back to your left hip. This completes 'Upward blow with elbow'.

You need not move your legs for the next elbow blow. Continue by lowering your right fist to your right hip as you twist your shoulders to your right and swing your left bent arm forward and inward. As your left elbow strikes forward at the envisaged attacker's chest region your fist is twisted so that the knuckles become uppermost and the fist is near to your breast-bone.

Implement 'Sideways blow with elbow' by moving your right foot directly to your left so that it becomes directly in front of, and some twenty inches away from, your left foot. Pivot outwards on the ball of your left foot as you twist your body to your left. The toes of your feet should be turned somewhat inward with legs well bent and knees turned slightly outward. Fold your arms loosely across your chest, look to your right and jab your right elbow horizontally to this direction into the supposed attacker's ribs. Concurrently retract your left fist to your left hip.

Finalise your actions by performing the fourth blow with

your left elbow. Start to accomplish this by pivoting around to your left on the ball of your right foot as you step backwards with your left bent leg. Look backwards over your left shoulder and immediately that you again stabilise your position poke your left elbow powerfully backwards as you twist your shoulders to your left.

RETREATING

Now try the same series of elbow blows while retreating from the hypothetical attacker.

Once again let's start in the position of left side Downward Block with left leg and arm forward. Step a large pace backward with your left leg as you withdraw your left fist to your left hip. Concurrently bend your right arm to bring your right elbow quickly forward and upward as the palm of your hand nears the right side of your neck.

Do not move your legs as you begin to move your left bent arm forward and inward. Sharply twist your shoulders to your right as you twist your left fist so that the knuckles become uppermost and the front of your fist is stilled when it is near to your breast-bone. At the same time move your right fist back to your right hip.

In preparation for 'Sideways blow with elbow' move your right foot directly to your left until it is in front of, and some twenty inches away from, your left foot. Twist about to your left on the ball of your right foot before turning your toes partially inwards as you well bend your legs and turn your knees somewhat outwards. Look to your right at the presumed attacker then fold your arms slackly across your chest, with the right one uppermost. Use a powerful contrary arm action by poking your right elbow horizontally forward to your right as you retract your left fist to your left hip. The movement of your right arm is stilled as the thumb of your right hand nears your right nipple.

Now conclude the set of elbow blows by performing 'Backward blow with elbow'. Pivot on the ball of your right foot to your left as you take back your left leg and twist your head to look to this direction. As soon as you regain a strongly balanced stance, in which you are facing the opposite direction to which you originally faced at the start of this four-set movement, move your left fist to your right. When your left fist nears your right shoulder swing your left elbow back to your left as you twist your shoulders to your left. Make the elbow blow and ensure that your left arm becomes motionless when your left fist is near to the left side of your body.

As usual you should become acclimatised to all the required actions by practising moving forward and backward across the practice area. The 'Backward blow with elbow' may be alternately horizontal or angled upward in order to prepare for the eventuality where you cannot successfully use one particular level of counter when the attacker is behind you.

Delivering a Kick

From the standpoint of self-defence the leg has many advantages over the arm. It is, of course, longer than the arm and would, therefore, probably compete with equal or greater effectiveness than the arm. In addition, if one is wearing shoes there is no doubt about the potentially heavy counter-blow which could thus be utilised. For this reason I recommend kicking actions as a 'long range' form of counter. This use of the lower limbs is particularly advantageous for women and the older more mature man.

I have respect for the sentiment of those who do not use anything but the fists when defending themselves, as formulated for the sport of boxing by the 8th Marquis of Queensberry. I am bound to observe, however, that anyone now following this sort of precept against the unscrupulous attacker would be at a grave disadvantage from the outset.

The main factor constantly to bear in mind when using

any of the following kicking actions is that your leg must firstly be bent with knee raised high before the leg is straightened.

Horizontal Front 'Snap' Kick

Stand upright with your feet shoulder width apart then clench your fists. Raise your arms in front of yourself and

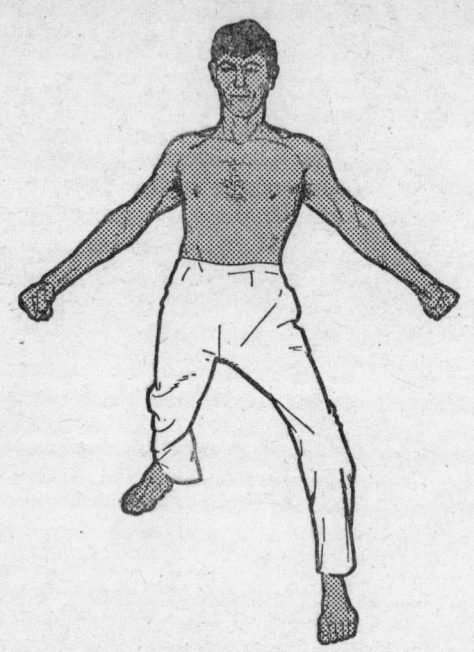

FIG. 58

cross them at the wrists so that the right arm is nearest to you. Step forward and outward on to your left bent leg as you flick your wrists outward and downward to their respective sides of your body. Stretch your right leg whilst keeping your back straight. This is the recommended stance to use while practising kicks to your front (Fig. 58).

Ensure that you keep your left leg bent with your left

foot planted firmly upon the floor and your back straight throughout the kicking actions.

Look directly forward as you bend your right leg so that your right knee is raised in front of your right hip. Stretch the lower part of your right leg forward so that you slowly kick the imaginary attacker in the region of his stomach

FIG. 59

with the ball of your right foot (Fig. 59). Once you have accomplished the kicking action bend your right leg before replacing the ball of your right foot back down upon the floor in its original position.

Perform ten kicking actions in slow motion then accomplish ten quick kicks.

The basis of this specific kicking action is that you remain in a static position firmly balanced upon your bent left leg.

High Front 'Snap' Kick

The aim of this technique is to deliver a head-high kick.

Take up the same starting position as in the technique just described. It is vital that your right knee is raised high into the air before the lower part of your leg is flicked upward.

FIG. 60

Well bend your right leg so that your right knee is brought close to your chest before flicking your right foot upward (Fig. 60). You should ensure that your back remains straight as there is a tendency toward leaning backward to gain height for the kicking action. If you mistakenly lean backward it will weaken your posture and could leave you open to a further possible attack (Fig. 61).

FIG. 61

Horizontal 'Thrust' Kick

The attacker may suddenly jump away during an attack
to nonplus you when you counter him by kicking out. He
may then intend to resume his attack by quickly advancing
again. In order to ensure that the attacker is not permitted
to avoid your counter-attack you can extend the range of
your leg by lunging forward at the last moment so that his
calculation of being a safe distance away is made incorrect.

The story is told of a peerless swordsman of 'old Japan'
who invariably avoided the edge or point of his adversary's
sword by a fraction before striking a blow in his turn. Another rival Samurai considered the other's great skill and
had a special sword made with a blade a little longer than
the prevailing length. When the two met in combat the
master swordsman as usual swayed away just enough seemingly to avoid the cut from his opponent's blade but was

instead wounded with the edge of the weapon. Whether this little story is fact or fiction the moral is still there as a guide.

Adopt the same stance as you did before practising the Horizontal Front 'Snap' Kick with your clenched fists near your sides and your bent left leg forward.

FIG. 62

Keep your back straight as you bend your right leg by bringing your right knee upwards in front of your right hip. Straighten your right leg by flicking your lower leg forward while keeping your toes pointed upwards. Imagine that you are lunging at the attacker with the ball of your foot striking his stomach. As you perform this kicking action stretch your right leg forward and then allow yourself to lose balance to the front (Fig. 62). When you lose balance your right foot is moved diagonally downward and outward onto the floor and replaced on the surface well in front of your left leg. You finalise this kicking action by bending your right leg while regaining a stable posture. It is important that your right foot performs the kicking movement a split second before you purposely lose your balance as otherwise the power of your kick is decreased.

High 'Thrust' Kick

After you have performed the horizontal kicking action with your right foot prepare to implement the High 'Thrust' Kick with your left foot.

Fully bend your left leg so that your left knee is raised in front of your chest then flick your left foot upwards so that you accomplish a head-high kicking action with your left foot while stretching your left leg. It is imperative that your back is kept straight and that you do not attempt to gain extra height for your kicking action, to the detriment of your balance, by leaning backwards. As soon as you have performed the kicking action allow your forward momentum to continue by lowering your left foot downwards and outwards when you regain a firmly balanced and wide stance, with your left bent leg in advance of your right leg.

If you have considerable space you can continue advancing by using your right leg to deliver the Horizontal Front Thrust Kick and then immediately follow this by using your left leg for the High 'Thrust' Kick. In limited space you merely turn about and practise the kicking actions to the reverse direction. It is a good plan to reverse the roles of your legs so that you can use either leg to kick horizontally or almost vertically with equal facility.

If you have the help of a partner he or she can help you considerably during training. If a coat is held or positioned in front of you, at a suitable height, you are able to add some measure of realism by kicking the article of clothing with a foot. This form of training is useful for improving many kicking actions.

Your partner can also help you to maintain a strong sense of balance while kicking forward. This can be achieved if a long belt is tied to your belt at the front. Your partner should stand holding one end of the belt and thus be in a position to tug at your belt just as you kick. By your partner's action you will be compelled momentarily to maintain your posture by retarding the forward movement of the middle part of your body against the pressure being exerted upon your belt. You can, of course, arrange some other contrivance to fit the requirements if you do not happen to be wearing belts.

Side 'Snap' Kick

Stand upright with your ankles pressed closely together and knees slightly bent. Position your lightly clenched hands in front of your chest (Fig. 63).

Now slightly twist your upper body to your right by with-

FIG. 63

drawing your right shoulder as you raise your right bent leg so that your right knee is in front of the right side of your chest. Kick your right foot upwards past your right side so that your right leg becomes almost straight. As soon as you perform the kicking action quickly bend your legs before again raising your right knee before flicking your right foot upward towards your right. Immediately replace your right foot upon the floor next to your left foot. Use your right foot ten times before using the same form of kicking action with your left leg.

You should get used to practising three consecutive actions by moving sideways firstly to your right then to your left. The object is to gain elasticity in your legs and hips by crossing one foot with the other so that your legs become crossed at the ankles before kicking out with the 'rear' leg.

Start by standing with your feet about shoulder width apart with your clenched hands in position in front of you. You should look to your right and twist your upper body to this direction with your right fist held in front of you and your left fist positioned near to the left side of your stomach. Move your left foot across the front of your right foot and replace it on the floor close to the outside of your right foot (Fig. 64). Raise your right knee high as you flick your right foot out from behind your left foot and perform a Side 'Snap' Kick. As soon as you make this kick replace your right foot upon the floor about a yard away from the inside of your left foot. Progress by moving your left foot to your right across the front of your right foot then quickly make the 'snap' kick with your right leg. After replacing your right foot upon the floor continue moving to your right by crossing your legs at the ankle before once again kicking with your right leg.

Once you have accomplished the three Side 'Snap' kicking actions when moving directly sideways to your right you should use your left leg to implement the kicking action when moving directly to your left.

Move your left fist in front of you, with your right fist

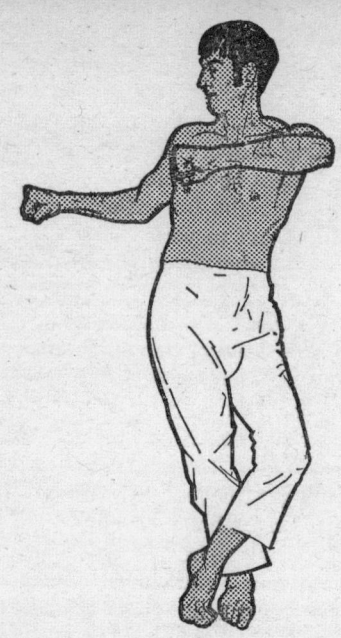

FIG. 64

positioned close to the right side of your stomach as you
twist your upper body and look directly to your left. Move
your right foot across the front of your left leg until it is
replaced upon the floor close to the outside of your left
foot. You then flick your left foot from behind your right
heel and perform the kicking action with your left foot.
Replace your left foot upon the floor some one yard distance away from the inside of your right foot before once
again moving your right foot to your left across the front
of your left foot.

Implement the kicking action with your left leg then
continue moving to your left, bypassing the front of your
left foot with your right foot. Make the third kicking action
with your left leg.

You should continue by moving alternately directly to

your right and then to your left until you gain some practical knowledge of the movements involved.

You can also obtain very useful training in the performance of Side 'Snap' Kick with the help of a partner.

Stand sideways to each other with your right side and your partner's left side inwards some four feet or so apart dependent upon your height. Clasp your partner's left hand with your right and position your hands at about shoulder-level height between you.

You should prepare to make the kicking action by crossing your feet at the ankles with your right foot behind your left. Make ten quick and consecutive Side 'Snap' Kicks with your right foot to a point near to your partner's left armpit. After you have completed your ten kicking actions your partner can accomplish ten kicking actions with his or her left foot. Simply both turn about to face the opposite direction and change your hand holds before resuming the kicking actions. You use your left leg while your partner uses the right leg.

Side 'Thrust' Kick

Stand upright with your feet positioned closely together then slightly bend your legs and position your clenched hands at the front of your body.

Well bend your right leg so that your knee is raised in front of your right hip. Straighten your right leg directly sideways to your right so that the leg and foot are parallel to the floor with the toes of your right foot pointed forward. You will probably find that you have to twist your left foot slightly outwards as you straighten your right leg. It is important that your right hip is moved forward and not back (Plate 3).

After you have replaced your right foot upon the floor close to the inside of your left foot slightly bend your legs before once again performing the kicking action with your right leg. You should accomplish ten kicking actions in slow motion with your right leg before exercising the kicking action by using your left leg an equal number of times.

It is best that you practise the kick in two distinct parts until you get used to the required actions.

Once you have become reasonably practised at using Side 'Thrust' Kick while standing still you should try out the technique while moving directly sideways.

Stand upright while keeping your feet spaced shoulder width apart and then twist your body slightly to your right. Position your lightly clenched hand in front of your right side and your left fist in front of your chest.

Step directly inwards with your left foot so that it traverses directly across the floor in front of your right foot and then replace your left foot on the floor close to the outside of your right foot. Now bend your right leg so that your right knee becomes raised in front of your right hip. Flick your right foot outwards so that the toes of your foot point directly forward as you straighten your right leg to make it parallel to the floor. After you have accomplished this kicking action bend your right leg and then replace your right foot upon the ground some twenty inches away from your left foot.

Continue by stepping inwards with your left foot until it traverses across the front of your right foot. Once your legs become crossed at the ankles make the kicking action as before with your right foot. After you have straightened your right leg, as though kicking the attacker's body with the sole of your right foot, replace your right foot upon the floor some twenty inches away from your left foot.

Make your third kicking action by stepping across the front of your right foot with your left foot before bending your right leg and implementing the kick with your right foot.

Now practise the three kicking actions while moving exactly to your left and using your left foot.

Twist slightly to your left as you position your loosely clenched left hand in front of your left hip and your right clenched hand in front of your stomach. Step inwards with your right foot past your left foot in the accepted way before kicking sideways to your left with your left foot. Return your left foot to the floor some twenty inches away from your right foot. Continue to move to your left by moving your right foot past the front of your left foot before kicking sideways with your left leg. Replace your left foot upon the floor then traverse your left foot with your right foot and implement the third kicking action with your left leg.

You should diligently practice darting directly to your left and then right while making the three set kicking actions.

As you get progressively more adept at the actions you can safely use larger movements so that you cover more ground, as it were. You should, however, be careful not to overreach yourself.

It is most important that you place the foot which you intend to kick with behind your other foot. This will entail a greater range of movement while ensuring that you kick sideways and consequently pave the way for increasing the suppleness of your leg and hip joints.

If you have the help of a partner you can clasp hands and use the kicking actions upon one another as I recommended in the technique of Side 'Snap' Kick.

There is a usual tendency not to raise the knee before kicking and this general fault is even more pronounced in Side 'Thrust' Kick. To train yourself always to raise your knee fix a string, rope or belt between two fixed objects some eighteen inches from the floor. If you stand close to the flimsy barrier which you have rigged-up and then practise kicking over it you will become used to raising your knee high into the air before kicking with your foot. Once you have become well versed in this type of activity there is no hitch in the compound kicking action which becomes one smooth quick movement.

Horizontal Backward Kick

This form of kicking action is aptly used if the attacker is closing with you from behind and you perceive him when he is still about a yard behind. Provided you have a split second warning you can utilise this kicking action against such an attacker. You can also combine this technique with other kicking actions as a combination counter-attack.

Stand upright with your feet positioned closely together and legs slightly bent. Raise your lightly clenched hands in front of your chest and twist your head to your right so that you can look to the direction behind your right shoulder. Raise your right knee outwards to your right and then straighten your right leg directly backwards. You should imagine that you deal the middle part of the attacker's body a blow with the sole of your right foot as your right leg becomes almost fully extended (Plate 4).

Once you have made the kicking action again bend your right leg before returning your right foot to the floor close to the inside of your left foot. Remember partially to bend your legs before again performing the kicking action with your right leg.

After you have executed ten kicking actions with your right leg use your left leg to make ten kicking actions.

Now combine the Horizontal 'Thrust' Kick with the Horizontal Backward Kick.

Start by adopting a stance with your right bent leg in advance of your left leg and position your lightly clenched hands in front of your chest. Raise your left knee into the air in front of your left hip then kick forward with your left foot as you straighten your left leg forward so that it becomes fully extended. As soon as you have delivered a kick with your left foot to the imagined attacker's middle sway forward on your right foot as you replace your left foot upon the floor. Continue by pivoting outwards to your left on the ball of your left foot as you twist about to the same direction so that you turn to face the opposite direction to which you originally faced. Stabilise your posture on your left leg as you well bend your right leg before kicking backwards with your right foot so that your right leg becomes parallel to the floor.

You should quickly replace your right foot upon the floor and then use the combined kicking action while moving to the opposite direction to which you were originally facing. As usual your object in training should be to gain a useful knowledge of the technique.

Round House Kick

This technique is very powerful and awkward to nullify in that the attacking foot evades a purely forward defence by an obliquely angled attack.

Start by adopting the left side style of Downward Block with bent left leg in advance of your straightened right leg. Raise your loosely clenched fists in front of you in a sparring position.

Well bend your right leg in such a way that your right knee is raised diagonally forward to your right in front of your right hip. Continue by pivoting outwards on the ball of your left foot to your left as you flick your right foot in a forward anti-clockwise action toward the supposed attacker's chin. Ensure that your right foot is turned slightly inwards to your left as you make the kick (Plate 5). Once you have accomplished the kicking action bend your right leg and return your right foot to the floor obliquely behind your left foot. You should try these actions some ten times.

Now take up the right side version of the Downward Block with your right leg in advance of your left leg. Once again assume the sparring position with your loosely clenched fists held in front of you. Well bend your left leg so that your left knee is moved diagonally outwards to your left in front of your left hip. Continue by flicking your left foot forward in a clockwise direction so that your foot is turned inwards as you administer the head-high kick. As soon as you have accomplished the kicking action bend your left leg and return your left foot to its original position upon the floor.

You should make ten kicking actions with your left foot.

It is helpful if you can get a partner to aid you in practising this kicking action.

You should both adopt the left side version of Downward Block with your bent leg in advance. Close to within a yard or so away from each other and then clasp your partner's right hand with your left hand. Your partner should help you maintain balance if needful. Slowly bend your right leg so that your right knee is moved outwards and upwards. Move your right foot forward and inward to rest your foot upon your partner's left shoulder. You should make the kicking action in slow motion many times before your partner uses the same type of movement by using the right leg and resting the right foot upon your left shoulder.

After practising the kick by using your right leg both take up the right side style of Downward Block with right leg in advance and you then bring your left foot to your partner's right shoulder some ten times. After you have practised the kicking actions in slow time afford your partner the opportunity to perform with the left leg.

It is imperative when performing the Round House Kick in bare feet that the foot is correctly positioned so that your toes do not become damaged through striking a relatively hard part of the attacker. The aim is to use the ball of your foot as the actual point of contact. This entails you to keep your big toe pressed back while your other toes are curved downwards.

You can practise Round House Kick with each leg alternately while standing stationary in order to gain elasticity in your hip and leg joint.

Stand upright with your feet close together and your loosely clenched hands positioned in front of you. Bend your right leg in such a way that your right knee is raised obliquely forward to your right. Pivot outwards slightly on the ball of your left foot as you twist your hips to your left and bring your right foot forward in a counter-clockwise action toward the hypothetical attacker's chin. Immediately bend your right leg before replacing your right foot on the floor close to your left foot.

Continue by bending your left leg so that your left knee is brought diagonally upwards to your left. Twist slightly to your right on the ball of your right foot as you twist your hips to your right. Concurrently move your left foot forward in a clockwise action to perform the kicking movement. Once you have made the kick quickly bend your left leg before replacing your left foot upon the floor close to your right foot.

You should perform this kicking action, using each leg alternately, for some twenty times upon each occasion that you practise.

Front Kick combined with Side 'Thrust' Kick

If you counter the attacker with a kicking action he may possibly jump back to avoid your oncoming foot. In order still to deliver a counter-blow you can use Side 'Thrust' Kick, with barely a perceptible pause, to the same direction with your other foot.

1ST METHOD

If you have the assistance of a partner he should stand facing you about a yard away and be prepared to take two or three steps backwards to avoid both of four kicking actions.

Take up the stance of Downward Block with your bent left leg forward. Raise your left fist in front of your chest. Well bend your left leg and then flick your left foot forward at stomach level. After you have used your left leg to perform a kicking action lunge forward and replace your left foot upon the floor as you intentionally lose balance.

Twist your left foot outwards and thus withdraw your left side so that your right side is nearest your partner. Well bend your right leg so that your right knee becomes raised in front of your chest. Straighten your right leg to perform Side 'Thrust' Kick exactly to the direction of your original advance (Fig. 65).

After you have completed the combined action reverse the roles of your legs. Adopt the right side version of Downward Block with your bent right leg in advance of your left. Raise your right fist until it is positioned in front of your chest. Bend your right leg so that your right knee is raised in front of your chest then straighten your leg by

FIG. 65

kicking forward at stomach level with your right foot. Lose balance to a forward direction as you replace your right foot on the floor diagonally in front of your left foot. Pivot outwards on your right foot as you well bend your left leg by raising your left knee in front of your chest. Straighten your left leg exactly to the direction of your original advance as you perform Side 'Thrust' Kick.

2ND METHOD

If you are faced by a wily attacker he may jump diagonally backwards to the side to avoid your first retaliatory kick rather than simply rely on moving backwards. In this event you can confound him in return by using Side 'Thrust' Kick to your side.

Stand facing your partner about a yard apart and assume

Downward Block with your bent left leg in front of your right. Move your left fist upwards until it is in front of your chest. Bend your left leg as you raise your left knee in front of your stomach before extending your left leg by kicking forward at stomach height with your left foot. Your partner should dodge your left foot by jumping well to his left and your right. Replace your left foot upon the floor diagonally in front of your right foot. Bend your right leg so that your right knee becomes raised in front of your chest. Now powerfully straighten your right leg outwards to your right, with the toes of your right foot pointed forward, so that your foot is parallel to the floor as you complete the kicking action.

After accomplishing the combined technique from the left side version of Downward Block adopt the right side style with your bent right leg in advance. Raise your right fist until it is in front of your chest. Well bend your right leg by raising your right knee in front of your chest then straighten your leg by kicking forward with your right foot at stomach level.

Lose balance to the front and replace your right foot on the floor diagonally in front of your left foot. Well bend your left leg by raising your left knee upwards in front of your chest. Kick your left leg outwards to your left so that the toes of your left foot point forward and the foot is parallel to the floor.

After practising the two methods of Front Kick coupled with Side 'Thrust' Kick individually dart about the practice area and use either method to meet your partner's form of avoidance. As always you should afford him the same chance to try out the moves.

It is noteworthy that Japanese Champions, such as Sensei Enoeda, perform these kicks with such power that an audible noise is made by the limbs abruptly straightening the material of the trousers.

Combining Defence with Counter-attack

Now that we have considered the defensive blocking actions and forms of counter-attack let's consider certain combinations of these two integral parts of self-defence. These further techniques are calculated to train your mind and body to function in harmony if you are under attack.

Rising Block—coupled with two counter-punches

The assumption is that the attacker will attempt to punch you in the face with his right fist.

Stand upright with your feet about shoulder width apart and loosely clenched hands by your sides. Step forward on to your left bent leg. Concurrently move your left fist to your left hip, palm uppermost, before punching your left fist diagonally upward some twelve inches in front of your right shoulder then twist your left fist so that the knuckles of your left hand are nearest to you and your forearm and fist form a 45 degree angle with the floor. Your upper body should be somewhat twisted to your right so that you are partially sideways to the imagined opponent with your left side nearest him and your right fist should be moved back to your right hip.

Now suddenly extend your left arm and punch forward with your left fist as though you intend punching the attacker upon the nose. You should keep your right shoulder back as you deliver this blow and fully expand your chest (Fig. 66). Follow this punch with your left fist with a right handed punch to his chest. Move your right fist horizontally forward as you twist your hips slightly to your left so that you come squarely to face the attacker. Once your right arm becomes almost fully extended twist your right fist so that the knuckles become uppermost just as the envisaged point of contact is made. At the same time withdraw your left fist to your left hip (Fig. 67).

It is essential that the twisting action of your upper body is closely synchronised with your right handed punch so that the power of your hips, stomach and upper body are all incorporated with the blow.

FIG. 66

Now resume your original position with lightly clenched hands by your sides and prepare to accomplish the actions on the other side, as it were.

Step forward on to your right bent leg as you make the Rising Block with your right arm and move your left fist to your left hip. Fully extend your right arm as you make a head-high forward punch with your right fist. Twist your right fist at the last moment so that your knuckles become uppermost and expand your chest while keeping your left shoulder back. Initiate the chest-level punching action with your left hand moving horizontally forward. As your left arm becomes straightened twist your hips slightly to your right so that you utilise the power of your body and twist

FIG. 67

your left fist in order that the knuckles become uppermost. Move your right fist back to your right hip as you make the final punching action.

You must again ensure that the twisting movement of your body coincides with the last punching action and that your whole power is used behind your punch as you turn squarely to your front.

You should implement this compound defensive and counter-attack action while moving both forward and backward in sets of three, in order that you become thoroughly well versed in the actions which are called for.

Knife-edge Block—coupled with a kick and punch
The presumption is that the attacker attempts to punch you in the chest with his right fist.

FIG. 68

You start by standing upright with your feet close together and hands by your sides. Straighten your right arm horizontally forward with fingers pointed toward the front and move your left hand over your extended right arm to a point near to your right ear. The palm of your left hand should be closest to your right ear (Fig. 68). Twist your right foot directly outwards as you well bend your right leg and glide your left foot directly forward in front of your right foot to assume the so-called 'back stance'.

Flick your opened left hand powerfully forward and slightly outward to a point some twelve to fifteen inches in front of your left shoulder as you sharply retract your opened right hand to your chest. You should imagine that you are knocking the attacker's lower right arm aside with the little-finger edge of your left hand as you sharply withdraw the little-finger edge of your right hand into contact with your breast-bone. Ensure that the fingers and thumbs of each hand are pressed closely together and both arms are bent.

Once you have knocked aside the assumed blow you are in a position to retaliate. Support your weight upon your bent right leg and bend your left leg so that your left knee is raised in front of your left hip. Flick your left foot forward as though you are kicking the assailant in the middle body. In bare feet the ball of your foot is used for this purpose (Fig. 69). As soon as you have made this kicking action replace your left foot diagonally downwards upon the floor. As you return your left foot to the surface change your stance by well bending your left leg as you twist your right foot forward so that you can take up the forward stance. You should now have a wide stance with your right leg and back kept straight with head up. Move your right hand back to your right hip in the usual way and form it into a fist.

Immediately upon stabilising your posture you are ready to make the final punching action to the chest. Move your right fist horizontally forward, with palm uppermost, and then just as your right arm is becoming straight twist your fist so that the knuckles become uppermost. Remember to tense your muscles as you deliver the blow.

Let's assume that the attacker attempts to punch you in the chest with his left fist. Resume your original position and prepare to use the counter actions starting with your right arm. Extend your left arm forward in line with your shoulder with fingers pointed forward and move your

FIG. 69

opened right hand to your left ear so that the palm of your
hand is nearest to your ear. Make certain that the fingers
and thumb of each hand are pressed closely into contact
with one another. Pivot outwards on the ball of your left
foot until your toes point directly to your left then well
bend your left leg outwards as you glide your right foot
directly forward until your right leg becomes almost
straight. Your weight should be mainly supported by your
left bent leg with your feet directly in line with, but at right
angles to, one another. Jerk your right lower arm sharply
forward and slightly downward as you withdraw your left
hand to your chest so that the little-finger edge of your
opened left hand becomes pressed against your breast-bone.
Still the movement of your right arm as soon as your hand

comes some twelve inches in front of your right shoulder when you have supposedly knocked the attacker's left arm aside with the little-finger edge of your unclenched right hand. Maintain your balance upon your bent left leg as you raise your right leg so that your right knee is brought in front of your right hip then jerk your lower right leg forward to make a stomach-level kick with your right foot. Withdraw your left hand in the form of a fist to your left hip.

After you have accomplished the kicking action return your right foot diagonally downwards to the floor and well bend your right leg as you twist your left foot forward. You now assume a forward stance with your right foot in advance of your left foot and feet reasonably widely spaced apart. As soon as you become well balanced punch forward at chest level with your left arm and twist your left fist so that the knuckles become uppermost as your arm becomes extended.

You should move forward and backward while implementing the defence and counter moves in the usual sets of three. At first you will probably find it wise to use slow and quite deliberate actions. This will make it feasible for you to gain fluidity of continuous movement. On no account should you attempt to move in a hurly burly fashion under the mistaken impression that technique can be safely penalised for the sake of speed.

Four blocking actions—coupled with punch

In the blocking actions which I have previously described we have considered single attacks and combined attacks which may require the use of two or three blocking actions with each of your arms alternately. In this present example the idea is that you make three consecutive blocking actions with your right arm then punch with your left fist followed by a further block with your right arm.

Apart from using the same arm with which to block you perform your whole arm movements from a static position in preparation for the time when you are forced to defend yourself against several blows with one of your arms without moving your feet.

Stand upright with your feet shoulder-width apart and arms hanging naturally by the respective sides of your body.

Step forward on to your bent right leg and implement Rising Block with your right arm as you move your left fist to your left hip. Once you have made Rising Block with your right arm prepare to make the Downward Block. Move your right fist, palm inwards, near to your left ear then flick your right arm across your body to the point above your right knee for the right side version of Downward Block. Now institute the third blocking action of Twisting Outside Block (chest level). Do this by moving your right fist back beyond your right ear with palm outwards before swinging your right lower arm forward and downward. The movement of your arm is stilled when your right fist becomes positioned in front of your right shoulder with palm nearest you.

Now punch directly forward with your left fist at chest level as you retract your right fist to your right hip. As soon as you have made this left handed punch move your right fist over your left arm toward your left ear then quickly perform Downward Block by flicking your right fist toward your right knee as you withdraw your left fist to your left hip.

Once you have become adept at the required actions gradually increase the speed and power of your arm movements. You should think of being under attack in the following sequence. A punch to your face, two punches to your body—you then retaliate with a punch and finally block a blow to your body.

You should now accustom yourself to use your left arm in a defensive role against a flurry of blows.

You are assumed to be standing with feet level in the normal upright posture. Step forward on to your bent left leg and use your left arm to perform the Rising Block while moving your right fist back to your right hip. Move your left fist near to your right ear then flick your lower arm and fist forward and downward near to your left knee to perform Downward Block. Continue by raising your left fist upwards diagonally behind your left ear then twist your left forearm forward and slightly downwards to make Twisting Outside Block (chest level). Follow this by punching forward at chest level with your right fist as you move your left fist back to your left hip. Finalise your actions by moving your left fist over your right arm to near your right ear before making Downward Block by flicking your left fist downward to near your left knee and concurrently withdraw your right fist to your right hip.

While I have recommended you to make the Downward Block in the usual manner, you should, when necessary, move your fist somewhat horizontally near to the front of your hip. This is particularly important when knocking aside a punch aimed at your middle body. If you also use a powerful twisting action of your hips great power can be incorporated in this defensive action. Sensei Keinosuke Enoeda (Black Belt 5th Dan), one-time all-Japan Karate Champion, greatly favours this type of blocking action for attacks aimed at the middle body because of the inherent power which can be utilised by the use of the hips and stomach (Fig. 70).

Downward Block—coupled with forward blow with elbow

The presumption in this dual action is that you step forward while blocking a kick to the area of your stomach with Downward Block and retaliate immediately with a forward elbow blow at close range.

Stand upright with your feet about shoulder width apart with your lightly clenched hands and arms hanging naturally by their respective sides. Raise your extended right arm horizontally in front of you then move your left fist over your right arm before stepping forward and outward on to your bent left leg while performing Downward Block with your left arm. Concurrently withdraw your right clenched hand to your right hip with palm uppermost.

FIG. 70

Now make a forward blow with your right elbow without moving your feet. Do this by swinging your right elbow forward and inward as though you intend striking the left side of the attacker's chest with the point of your elbow. You should twist your forearm and still the movement when your right fist is near to your breast-bone with knuckles uppermost (Fig. 71).

Resume your starting position with feet shoulder width apart. Extend your left arm in front of you then bring your right fist over your left arm before stepping forward upon your bent right leg as you accomplish Downward Block with your right arm. At the same time withdraw your left fist to your left hip with palm uppermost. Carry on by using your left elbow to deal the presumed attacker a blow against the right side of his chest without moving your feet. Your left elbow should be swung forward and inward and your left fist should become stationary when it nears your breastbone with knuckles uppermost.

Let's now consider the two actions when you are moving forward and then backward.

Again start in the normal upright position with clenched hands by your sides. Extend your right arm horizontally forward then bring your left arm over your right arm so that the palm of your left fist is brought close to your right

FIG. 71

ear. Step forward and slightly outward upon your left bent leg as you make a strong Downward Block with your left arm. Coincidentally move your right fist back to your right hip with palm uppermost. As soon as you have effected the blocking action twist your right elbow forward and inward to strike the envisaged attacker's chest. Your hips should be twisted to your left as an aid to your elbow blow. At the completion of this action your right arm should be fully bent with right fist situated close to your breast-bone with knuckles uppermost.

Progress by straightening your left arm horizontally forward before moving your right fist over your left arm with palm nearest to your left ear. Step forward and somewhat outwards upon your right bent leg then achieve a powerful Downward Block with your right arm. Withdraw your left fist to your left hip with palm of the hand uppermost. Twist your hips to your right then swing your left elbow forward and inward at chest level and freeze your actions when your left fist nears your breast-bone.

Start to complete the third compound action by extending your right arm horizontally forward and move your left fist into position by your right ear. Step forward and partially outward upon your left bent leg and make the Downward Block with your left arm. Simultaneously retract your right fist to your right hip with palm uppermost. As soon as you have accomplished the blocking action twist your hips while swinging your right elbow forward and inward at chest level and halt your actions as your right fist nears your breast-bone.

Now momentarily maintain your final pose before beginning to retreat. Stretch your left arm horizontally forward then bring your right fist over your left arm with palm nearest to your left ear. Step backwards with your left foot as you well bend your right leg and institute Downward Block with your right arm while withdrawing your left fist to your left hip. Swing your left elbow forward and inward until your left fist nears your breast-bone.

Extend your right arm horizontally forward and bring your left fist over near to your right ear. Step a large pace backwards with your right foot as you allow your left leg to become well bent and achieve Downward Block with your left arm. As soon as you make the blocking action with your left arm withdraw your right fist to your right hip. Swing your right elbow forward and inward at chest level so that your right arm becomes fully bent with right fist close to your breast-bone.

Straighten your left arm forward and move your right fist to your left ear before making Downward Block with your right arm. Withdraw your left fist to your left hip. Finalise the three compound actions when retreating by using your left elbow to deliver the chest level blow.

As usual you should move backward and forward across the practice area so that you become thoroughly used to the requirements of this compound action.

Two blocking actions—coupled with three blows

It is of foremost importance to train the mind and body to act in unison when defending yourself. Unless the mind is purposefully trained in instructing the body to accomplish several techniques in a short space of time, there is a real risk of defending yourself haltingly when the attacker uses a flurry of blows.

You make only minute movements with your feet during the performance of the five technique called for. Start by standing with your feet extra widely spaced apart with toes pointed partially inward and legs bent with knees turned outward in the stance of KIBA DACHI. Ensure that your back is kept straight with head level. Your clenched hands should be positioned some twelve inches from the respective sides of your body (Fig. 72).

Pivot outward to your left on the heel of your left foot so that the toes of your foot point directly to your left and twist your upper body to face this direction. Your left leg should be fairly straight with right bent leg supporting the major part of your weight in the 'back stance'. Simultaneously tuck your left fist, with knuckles uppermost, under your right armpit, then flick your left fist outwards to your left so that you achieve the Inside Block. Your left fist should be in alignment with the front of your left shoulder with knuckles turned outwards (Fig. 73).

Now prepare to make Inside Block with your right arm. Swivel to your right on the heels of your feet so that your right foot points directly to your right and your left foot points forward. Your right leg should be partially straightened while your left leg becomes bent when you adopt the 'back stance'. At the same time insert your right fist under your left arm with knuckles uppermost before flicking your right fist outwards to your right to make Inside Block. Your right fist should become stilled when your fist is level

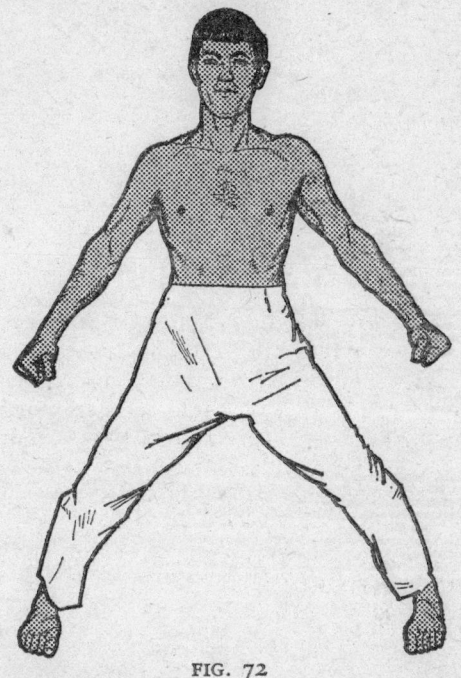

FIG. 72

with your right shoulder with knuckles twisted outward (Fig. 74).

Continue by making a backward blow with your left elbow without moving your feet. Do this by cupping the palm of your left fist with your right hand before poking your left elbow powerfully backward past your left side. The palm of your left fist should be kept uppermost as the blow is made.

FIG. 73

Once you make the backward blow with your left elbow get ready to use the little-finger edge of your left hand. Swivel around to your left on the heels of your left foot and right foot so that your left foot points to your left while your right points forward. You should adopt the 'back stance' with right leg well bent. Concurrently extend your left arm as you straighten your unclenched left hand to your left, with fingers and thumbs pressed together, while withdrawing your right fist to your right hip. Imagine you use the little-finger edge of your left hand with which to strike the blow. Your hand should be made motionless immediately upon your straightened arm becoming level with the front of your left shoulder (Fig. 75).

Your next action is to punch forward with your right fist without again moving your feet while maintaining 'back stance'. Withdraw your left hand, in the form of a fist, sharply to your left hip as you punch powerfully forward at chest level with your right fist.

Complete the compound action by pivoting on the heel of your left foot so that you twist to your right and revert to your original KIBA-DACHI stance,

You should also substitute left for right where necessary so that you accomplish the technique on the other side, as it were. This means that you twist to your right and make Inside Block with your right arm and then twist to your left to make Inside Block with your left arm. You then make a backward blow with your right elbow followed by an edge of hand blow with the little-finger edge of your unclenched right hand. You complete the actions by punching forward at chest level with your left fist.

FIG. 74

FIG. 75

Four blocking actions—coupled with four blows

This is a further series of blocking and counter-attacking actions devised to acclimatise the mind in instructing the body to accomplish several separate fighting actions in a short space of time. A further progressive step in this vital training is that some of the actions are performed on the move, as it were, so that strict control must be exercised by you over all of your body movements.

Stand in the normal upright posture with your loosely clenched hands positioned by their respective sides. Point the toes of your left foot directly to your left as you move your left foot some twelve inches to this direction and bend your right leg so that you assume 'back stance'. Simultaneously move your left fist with knuckles uppermost to a point under your right armpit before flicking your left fist to your left and moving your right fist to your right hip. You should imagine that you are blocking a horizontal blow with the thumb edge of your left wrist.

Now move your left foot outwards some few inches as you pivot inward on the heel of your right foot when you become able to bend your left leg and take up the forward stance. Punch powerfully forward with your right fist at chest level while moving your left fist sharply back to your left hip.

The actions now call for you to turn about to your right while implementing Downward Block with your right arm. After having performed the horizontal punching action with your right fist move your fist near to your left ear. Pivot around on your feet so that you turn completely about to your right so that your body is twisted through 180 degrees. When you have made this 'about turn' move your right fist diagonally downward across the front of your body to make the powerful action of Downward Block. It is important to regain balance quickly upon effecting this change of position and to still the movement of your right fist when it is above your right knee. Ensure that you adopt the 'forward stance' with your right leg well bent and back kept straight. Punch forward with your left fist in a powerful horizontal blow as you withdraw your right fist to your right hip.

Twist to your left so that you come to face the same direction as you originally faced. Allow your left leg to become straightened and bend your right leg in order that you adopt the 'back stance' with your weight mainly supported on your right bent leg. Concurrently unclench your hands while bringing your left palm near to your left ear before making Knife-edge Block with the lower part of your left arm.

Now make a stomach-level kick with your right foot. Do this by bending your right leg so that your right knee is raised in front of you then flick your right foot forward so that you imagine that you are kicking with the ball of the foot. Allow yourself to lose balance after making the kick and repace your right foot upon the floor well in advance of, and to the side of, your left foot. Stabilise your position in the forward stance with right leg well bent as soon as practicable.

Ascertain that you keep your back straight with hips pushed forward and look horizontally forward. Punch powerfully to your front with your left fist while moving your right fist back to your right hip.

Now complete your eighth action by turning to your left to make Knife-edge Block. Unclench your hands and move your hands so that the palm of your left hand becomes positioned by the right side of your neck with your right arm and hand extended in front of you at shoulder level. Advance your left foot sideways to your left and adopt 'back stance' so that the majority of your weight is borne by your right bent leg and you turn to face to your left. As you take up the 'back stance' execute the Knife-edge Block with the lower part of your left arm and move your opened right hand speedily back to the correct position by the middle of your chest.

You should try out these movements on the other side by substituting left for right where necessary.

Two blocking actions—coupled with three blows

This is a further five-set series of moves, with the essential difference to the one recently outlined that you now accomplish the blocking and counter actions while moving forward and backward across the area in which you are practising.

Stand upright with your arms hanging naturally with lightly clenched hands by your sides. Straighten your left arm forward and bend your right arm as you move your right fist diagonally beyond your right ear with palm facing outward and withdraw your right shoulder. Step forward and slightly outwards upon your bent right leg. Make the Outside Front Block (chest level) with your right arm by flicking your right fist inward and slightly downward. The movement of your right fist is stilled as it becomes positioned in line with the front of your right shoulder with knuckles twisted forward. Concurrently retract your left fist to your left hip.

You continue by making Sideways Elbow Blow by turning your right side nearest to the presumed attacker. Do this by moving your right foot inward to the left so that you place it upon the floor directly in front of, and at some twenty-four inches from, your left foot. You should not remove your left foot from the floor but merely pivot outward upon your foot when you twist your upper body to face to the left. Fold your arms across your chest, as though you are loosely hugging yourself, with your bent right arm above your left bent arm. The knuckles of your fists should be uppermost as you twist your head to look over your right shoulder at the envisaged attacker. Well bend your legs to adopt the stance of KIBA-DACHI with toes turned in, knees twisted outward and back kept straight. Make a powerful sideways elbow blow to your right at chest level by thrusting your right elbow outward. The movement of your right forearm is halted when the thumb of your right fist nears your right nipple. Concurrently withdraw your left fist to your left hip, with palm uppermost, as you tense the whole of your body when the blow is implemented.

The presumption is that after having poked the attacker in the ribs with your right elbow he will recoil somewhat so that you can extend the range of your counter-attack by utilising your right fist. Your feet should not be moved and your right arm is merely straightened so that you deliver a sideways blow, at head height, with the back of your fist. As you straighten your right arm horizontally sideways to your right twist your fist so that your thumb becomes uppermost. Flick your fist backward so that the knuckles are brought towards the back of your right wrist. The knuckles of your right fist are intended to be used to rap against the attacker's face (Plate 6).

Continue by opening your right hand as you twist your left foot forward while stepping outwards with your right foot to adopt 'forward stance' as you well bend your right leg. As you twist to your right in order squarely to face to your front keep your back straight. Retract your right hand sharply to your hip and punch forward at chest level with your left fist.

Finalise the series of actions by moving your right fist over your extended left arm to near to your left ear before flicking your right fist obliquely downward toward your right knee in Downward Block. At the same time move your left fist back to your left hip.

Bring into effect the second series of the five technique. Raise your extended right arm horizontally in front of your chest as you bend your left arm while moving your left fist, palm outwards, diagonally behind your left ear. Step a large pace forward and outward upon your bent left leg as you flick your left fist forward and inward to perform Outside Front Block (chest level) with your left arm. Your arm action is stilled as soon as your left fist becomes positioned in front of your left shoulder with palm nearest to your shoulder. Coincidentally pull back your right fist to your right hip.

Move your left foot to your right so that you replace it on the floor directly in front of and some twenty-four inches away from your right foot. As you take up the position of KIBA-DACHI, by well bending your legs, you should be at right angles to the hypothetical attacker with your left side nearest him. Twist your head to your left as you look over your left shoulder and loosely fold your arms across your chest with the left bent arm uppermost. Ensure that you are strongly balanced with back straight as you jab your left elbow to your left at chest level with knuckles uppermost. Stop the movement when the thumb of your left fist nears the left side of your chest and sharply retract your right fist to your right hip.

Straighten your left arm outward to your left as you flick the back of your left fist into contact with the supposed attacker's face.

Open your left hand as you step outwards with your left foot and adopt the 'forward stance' with left leg well bent and back straight. Ascertain that you squarely face your front with feet pointed forward and back kept straight. Punch forcibly forward at chest level with your right fist and return your left fist speedily to your left hip.

Complete the second series of the five technique. Straighten your left arm forward as you bend your right arm and position your right fist obliquely behind your right ear. Step a large pace forward and outward upon your bent right leg as you flick your right fist forward and slightly downwards to achieve Outside Front Block (chest level). Retract your left fist to your left hip.

Move your right foot to your left, directly in front of your left foot, and adopt KIBA-DACHI stance as you twist to your left. Twist your head so that you look at the presumed attacker over your right shoulder. Fold your arms slackly across your body with your bent right arm uppermost and make the sideways blow with your right elbow as you retract your left fist to your left hip. Your right fist stops moving as it nears the right side of your chest.

Extend your right arm as you flick the knuckles of your right fist backwards at head height.

Open your right hand as you step outward upon your right foot and adopt the 'forward stance' with your right leg well bent. Keep your back straight and punch forcefully forward with your left fist as you move your right fist back to your right hip.

Bring your right fist over your left arm to your left ear. Make the Downward Block with your right arm by moving your right fist diagonally downward to your right knee. At the same time move your left fist back to your left hip.

After gaining a sound knowledge of practising the three sets of five technique when moving forward try out the same moves when retreating. At a later juncture move forward and backward across the practice area while utilising the compound technique.

'Sparring'

Up to now in this book the emphasis has been placed upon Karate technique which can be practised by yourself without the help of a partner. While this solitary training forms an integral part of basic training for Karate it is also equally vital now to obtain the help of a partner for bringing more realism to your training.

The first essential in this form of training is to accomplish the technique in slow motion as correctly as possible. On no account should a feeling of competition exist which shows itself as unexpected punches, changing direction of blow or unduly powerful actions. The whole aim of training is gradually to develop the attribute of blocking and retaliating with a counter-blow without getting flurried.

If you both wish to wear some form of protective padding on the lower forearm to avoid any possible bruising when strongly blocking each other's attack no harm is done. Failing this precaution you should use reasonably controlled actions. There is no reason why you should risk bruised wrists and forearms, for the sake of bravado, unless you intend to engage in Karate over an extended period and wish therefore to toughen these parts of your arms. After all, I think it logical to assume, irrespective of the outcome of an attack upon the person, that the defender would not generally be called upon to defend himself with more than a dozen blocking actions before the fight was ended one way or another.

Rising Block against punch to face
This blocking technique and the one immediately following are practised in sets of three, advancing and retreating, in order to acclimatise the exponent of Karate safely to nullify punches. It is of the utmost importance that you both keep your backs straight throughout the whole following changes of position.

You should stand facing your partner at arm's length apart before he adopts the left side version of Downward Block with his bent left leg in advance. His right fist should be held in readiness at his right hip while you stand with your feet shoulder width apart with arms hanging naturally by your sides.

Your partners should prepare to step a large pace forward on to his right bent leg when he delivers an angled punch directly toward your nose with his right fist and he retracts his left fist to his left hip. For his part he must move his fist directly toward your nose while ensuring that he keeps the little-finger edge of his wrist and forearm to his right side until his right fist is well on the way to your nose. If he does not do this his fist will tend to wave about and the punch will not be made in the accepted manner.

As your partner begins to step forward upon his bent right leg with the intention of literally punching you on the nose with his right fist you must adopt your counter actions.

Step a large pace backward upon your right leg as you bend your left leg. Move your left hand toward your left hip while forming it into a fist with palm uppermost. Make a diagonal punching action with your left fist so that it traverses the front of your body, roughly from your left hip to the front of your forehead, while twisting your fist so that the palm is twisted forward.

Your aim is to knock your partner's right wrist upwards with the little-finger edge of your left wrist so that you prevent him punching you upon the nose by using Rising Block. Your lower left arm and fist should be at an angle of 45 degrees to the surface at the completion of the blocking action. At the same time as you block with your left arm withdraw your right fist to your right hip (Fig. 76).

Immediately after blocking your partner's right fist with your left forearm prepare to deflect his left fist by using your right forearm.

Your partner should step an extra pace forward on to his bent left leg as he starts to aim a left-handed punch at your nose. Withdraw your left leg a large pace as you well bend your right leg. Move your right fist diagonally upwards, from right to left, so that you propel his left wrist upwards by contacting it with the little-finger edge of your right wrist in the prescribed method of Rising Block. At the same time take your left fist back to your hip (Fig. 77).

Your partner now prepares to make his third and final punching action with his right fist as he steps forward on

FIG. 76

to his bent right leg. As he moved forward withdraw your right leg in an exaggerated pace as you well bend your left leg. Punch diagonally upwards with your left fist as you knock his right wrist upward with the little-finger edge of your left wrist as you perform Rising Block (Fig. 78).

When you have accomplished the three blocking actions it is opportune to reverse roles with your partner by aiming the three set punches directly at his nose while he retreats and uses Rising Block. He should stand upright with his feet shoulder width apart and arms hanging naturally by his sides. You should take up the left side stance of the

FIG. 77

Downward Block and prepare to step forward upon your bent right leg while aiming a right-handed punch to your partner's nose. (You must both remember to keep your backs straight throughout the changes of position.)

FIG. 78

145

As you step forward upon your bent right leg your partner moves his left fist to his left hip while moving his right leg in a large pace backwards. When you punch forward with your right fist he executes Rising Block with his left arm in order to prevent your right fist from reaching his face. He then moves his right fist to his right hip.

I must reiterate that it is of the utmost importance that you both keep your backs straight throughout the whole following changes of position.

You continue by advancing your bent left leg with the intention of punching his face with your left fist. He takes back his left leg as he bends his right leg and makes Rising Block with his right arm. When he knocks your left wrist upwards due to the little-finger edge of his right wrist being twisted he makes a contrary-type action with his left fist being withdrawn to his left hip.

Begin to make your final attacking action by stepping forward upon your bent right leg before aiming your right fist at your partner's nose. Immediately that you step forward your partner withdraws his right leg as he makes Rising Block by knocking your right wrist upwards with the twisting action of his left wrist. He moves his right fist back to his right hip. This completes the compound actions.

Both you and your partner will probably find it difficult to judge the exact distance for punching and positioning and the only way quickly to overcome this is continuously to move back and forth across the practice area.

The main mistake to avoid is to make quite sure that you both keep your backs straight and do not allow your upper bodies to become inclined forward at any stage of the movements. Another error, in trying to be too co-operative, is purposely to veer your punches to the side of your partner's face instead of aiming directly at the nose. This does not help as it only gives a false sense of security and makes correct blocking actions impossible.

Outside Block (chest level) against punch to chest

It is again best that this blocking action is practised in sets of three with you using the blocking action at first before changing roles with your partner so that you can practise punching while he defends.

Stand in the normal upright position with clenched hands positioned by your sides and ask your partner to assume the left side stance of Downward Block with his bent left leg in advance.

Your partner should get ready to move his right leg forward in advance of his left leg before punching directly at your breast-bone with his right fist as he well bends his right leg. He moves his left fist back to his left hip. You should extend your right arm forward as you move your left fist, with palm outward diagonally behind your left ear and bend your left arm. When your partner punches at your chest with his right fist step a large pace backward with your right leg and bend your left leg. Twist your left arm inwards and slightly downwards, as you twist your fist, in order to propel his right fist inwards by sharply contacting his right fist with the little-finger edge of your left wrist. Freeze the movement of your left fist when your fist is level with the front of your left shoulder. Simultaneously sharply move your right fist back to your right hip (Fig. 79).

Your partner should now contemplate moving his left leg in advance of his right as he returns his right fist to his right hip and punches forward with his left fist aimed at your breast-bone.

Stretch your left hand forward as you bend your right arm and move your right fist diagonally behind your right ear with palm turned outward. Take your left leg a large pace backward as you bend your right leg. When your partner punches forward with his left fist aimed at the centre of your chest, quickly twist your right arm forward and inward. As you twist your right fist so that the knuckles become twisted forward you become able to knock your partner's left wrist inward with the little-finger edge of your right wrist. The movement of your right fist should cease when it is exactly in front of, and level with, your right shoulder. Coincidentally move your left fist back to your left hip.

Your partner should finalise his third punching action by stepping forward upon his bent right leg with the aim of punching at your chest with his right fist. Move your right leg a large pace backward as you stretch your right arm forward and bend your left leg. Bend your left arm and

FIG. 79

move your left fist diagonally behind your left ear with palm facing outward. Quickly twist your left arm inwards and slightly downwards so that you divert your partner's right fist by knocking his right wrist inward with the little-finger edge of your left wrist. Simultaneously withdraw your right fist to your right hip.

This completes the third blocking action.

On no account should you make tiny movements with the arm which you use to block for the sake of gaining speed. You must always endeavour to achieve as great a range of movement as possible, within the limits of safety, in order to generate the required power. This means that the blocking action must be executed at tremendous speed if you are attacked.

Now reverse roles with your partner so that you do the punching action while he does the blocking action.

Your partner should stand upright and his feet shoulder width apart with clenched hands by his sides. You should take up the left side style of Downward Block with your bent left leg in advance. Your aim is to step forward upon your right leg, then bend it, as you aim a right-handed punch exactly at the middle of his chest. Your partner moves his left fist diagonally behind his left ear, with palm outwards, as he bends his left arm. He should step back with his right leg while stretching his right arm forward. As you punch forward with your right fist at chest level you withdraw your left fist to your left hip. Your partner must swing his left arm inward and slightly downward so that the little-finger edge of his left wrist contacts your right wrist and knocks it inwards. His right fist should be withdrawn to his right hip.

Continue by advancing forward on to your bent left leg before punching at your partner's chest with your left fist. Your partner ought to withdraw his left leg as he stretches his left arm forward. He bends his right leg and arm while positioning his right fist diagonally behind his right ear with palm facing outward. He quickly twists his bent right arm inward and slightly downward so that the outside edge of his right wrist contacts the same part of your left wrist and propels it inward. He stops the action of his right arm when his right fist is level with the front of his right shoulder. His left fist should concurrently be withdrawn to his left hip.

You start to complete the last of your three punching actions by stepping forward upon your bent right leg preparatory to aiming a right-handed punch at your partner's chest. As you make the punching action your left fist should be moved back to your left hip. Your partner stretches his right arm forward as he bends his left arm while moving his left fist diagonally behind his left ear with palm outwards.

He should withdraw his right leg as he twists his bent left arm inward and slightly downward so that the outside of his left wrist contacts the same part of your right wrist and thus knocks the lower part of your right arm inwards. At the same time he retracts his right fist to his right hip. This ends the compound technique.

In order to become thoroughly well versed in the two roles you should both move back and forth across the practice area upon many separate occasions.

Rising Block—coupled with two elbow blows

This particular compound technique is another defence devised for use against the attacker who attempts to punch you on the nose.

In order to practise this technique get your partner to adopt the Downward Block stance with his bent left leg in advance and right fist positioned at his right hip with palm uppermost. Stand about four feet away in the normal upright posture with your unclenched hands positioned by your sides. Your partner should move his bent right leg forward in advance of his left leg as he attempts to punch you on the nose with his right fist. When he makes this punching action he ought to retract his left fist to his left hip.

As your partner attempts to punch you upon the nose with his right fist step forward upon your bent left leg and make this rather unusual style of Rising Block by bending your advanced left leg as you make the blocking action with your slightly bent *right* arm. Immediately that you have blocked your partner's right fist with Rising Block prepare to use two blows with your elbows. Swing your left elbow horizontally forward and inwards as you twist your hips and shoulders to your right to poke your left elbow gently into his ribs on the right side of his chest (Fig. 80).

The movement of your elbow should be stilled when your left fist is brought near to your breast-bone with knuckles uppermost. Make an upward blow with your right elbow towards your partner's chin while twisting your hips slightly to your left. At the completion of this last elbow blow your right arm should be fully bent with the palm of your right fist positioned close to your right ear (Fig. 81).

Now try out the actions when your partner aims his left fist at your nose. Step a small pace forward upon your bent

FIG. 80

right leg and perform the Rising Block with your slightly bent left arm. Simultaneously move your right hand to your right hip in the form of a fist with palm uppermost. Return your left fist to your left hip as you make a forward elbow blow with your right elbow by twisting your elbow forward and inwards. Still the actions when your right fist is near to your breast-bone with knuckles uppermost. Complete your actions by moving your right fist back to your right hip as you make an upward elow blow with your left elbow so that you almost strike your partner's chin. Still this last

FIG. 81

action as your arm becomes fully bent with the palm of your left clenched hand near to your left ear.

Once you have achieved some fluidity in accomplishing the compound actions try them out in sets of three when you are advancing or retreating. At the beginning of training you should try out the moves in slow motion while you move forward and your partner retreats in order to achieve synchronisation in timing.

Let's clarify in advance the initial actions which your partner will need to make. He should start his moves by adopting downward block with his bent left leg and left arm in advance with his clenched right hand positioned by his right hip. He should move his left leg in a large backward step, by-passing his right leg and then as he stabilises his change of position he should bend his right leg and let fly with his right fist at your nose as he retracts his left fist with palm uppermost.

Stand opposite your partner at a distance of about a

yard apart then both make Downward Block. Your partner should perform the left-side style of Downward Block with his bent left leg and left arm in advance while you execute the right side version of Downward Block with your bent right leg and right arm in advance.

Begin by advancing your left leg as your partner moves his left leg backwards and makes to punch you on the nose with his right fist. Prevent his right fist from striking your face by using Rising Block with your slightly bent right arm as you move your left fist back to your left hip. Continue by swinging your left elbow forward and inwards so that it lightly contacts the right side of his chest as you return your right fist to your right hip. Make an upward elbow blow with your right elbow toward the point of his chin while moving your left fist back to your left hip.

Your partner should continue his actions by withdrawing his right leg in an extra large pace before trying to punch you on the nose with his left fist as he withdraws his right fist to his right hip. As your partner attempts to punch your face with his left fist advance your bent right leg in front of your left leg and make Rising Block with your slightly bent left arm. Move your left fist back to your left hip while swinging your right elbow horizontally forward and inward so that you lightly brush the left side of his chest with the point of your right elbow when your right fist is brought near to your breast-bone with knuckles uppermost. Return your right fist to your right hip with palm uppermost as you thrust your left elbow towards his chin while fully bending your left arm and positioning the palm of your clenched left hand near to your left ear.

Your partner ought to continue moving backwards by withdrawing his left leg in an exaggerated pace before trying to punch you upon the nose with his right fist. When your partner prepares to punch your face with his right fist move your bent left leg forward and make Rising Block with your partially bent right arm. Return your right fist to your right hip as you make an horizontal twisting action with your left elbow to the right side of your partner's chest. Move your left fist back to your left hip and make the upwards elbow blow with your right elbow being brought near to your partner's chin. This completes the three-set technique when you are moving forward.

Now let's outline the compound technique when your partner advances and you retreat. His role is to adopt the left side stance of Downward Block and then to make three 'stepping punches' beginning with his right leg and right fist.

You should stand facing your partner about four feet away from him with your arms hanging naturally at your sides. As he steps forward upon his bent right leg and prepares to punch you upon the nose with his right fist withdraw your right leg and make Rising Block with your partially bent right arm. At the same time bend your advanced left leg and stabilise your position as you retract your left fist to your left hip. Make the forward horizontal blow with your left elbow and then accomplish the upward blow with your right elbow as you move your left fist back to your left hip.

Your partner continues his advance upon his bent left leg as he punches forward at your face with his left fist. Take back your left leg as you return your right fist to your right hip and make Rising Block with your slightly bent left arm. Move your left fist back to your left hip and make the horizontal elbow blow with your left elbow while again returning your right elbow to your right hip.

The last compound action begins with your partner advancing upon his bent right leg as he punches forward with his right fist. You start your counter measures by moving your right leg an abnormal pace backwards as you execute Rising Block with your right arm while quickly retracting your left fist to your left hip. Make the forward twisting action of your left elbow supposedly to strike the right side of his chest as you move your right fist back to your right hip. Finalise your actions by making the upward blow with your right elbow and move your left fist back to your left hip.

Twisting Outside Block (chest level) coupled with backward elbow blow

In this technique the attacker attempts to punch you in the chest with his fist which you block before twisting about and jabbing him in the ribs with the elbow of your other arm.

Request your partner to take up the left side style of Downward Block and to prepare to step forward upon his bent right leg before aiming his right fist at your breastbone. You should stand facing him with your arms hanging naturally by your sides. Bend your right arm while upraising your right fist, with palm outwards, diagonally behind your right ear. Step forward upon your bent right leg and swing your right arm forward and slightly downwards so that you contact the inside of his right wrist with the little-finger edge of your right wrist and propel his right arm outwards. At the same time withdraw your left fist to your left hip (Plate 7).

As soon as you prevent your partner's right fist from striking your chest prepare to make your counter blow with your left elbow. Make a 'left about turn' by twisting your body to your left and step backwards with your left leg and place your left foot upon the floor between your partner's feet. Sharply twist your hips to your left and make a backward blow with your left elbow so that you could poke your left elbow powerfully into the ribs on the left side of your partner's chest. The palm of your left fist should be kept uppermost with your fist kept close to the left side of your chest (Fig. 82).

Once you have become proficient at performing the block with your right arm and counter-blow with your left elbow reverse your actions.

In order to help you your partner should take up the right side stance of Downward Block preparatory to stepping forward upon his bent left leg before attempting to strike the middle of your chest with his left fist. Upraise your bent left arm and position your left fist, with palm outwards, diagonally behind your left ear. Twist your bent

FIG. 82

left arm forward and inward so that you bring the little-
finger edge of your left wrist into contact with the thumb
edge of his left wrist and knock his lower arm outwards.
Perform a 'right about turn' by twisting to your right as
you step backwards with your right leg and place your right
foot on the floor between his feet. Swivel your hips to your
right as you pretend to drive your right elbow backwards
into his ribs on the right side of his chest.

You should diligently study the actions which are called
for so that you gain the ability to twist suddenly about to
deal the attacker a sharp blow with your elbow.

From some aspects it is not safe purposely to turn your
back to the attacker. However, if you are partially sideways
to the attacker after blocking his punch, or some other factor has momentarily brought about this positioning, this
type of technique is aptly used. It often happens in the
hurly-burly of a fight that you become twisted partially

around and if you are proficient at dealing the attacker a backwards blow it does help in your overall defence.

After making this retaliatory blow you can quickly slip away before facing the attacker again or you can follow up with a Backward Kick, which is described elsewhere in this book, after your elbow strike has made him recoil somewhat.

Twisting Outside Block (chest level)—coupled with 'chop' and punch

In this compound action you are presumed to be attacked with a straight punch to your chest. You block this punch with your lower arm and then respond with a cut from the edge of the same hand to his neck before delivering a straight punch to his chest with your other hand.

To enable you to practise the defence your partner should take up the right side stance of Downward Block with his right leg and arm in advance. His role is then to step forward upon his bent left leg and to aim his left fist at your chest in an effort to punch your breast-bone as he moves his right fist back to his right hip. Upraise your bent right arm so that your fist is situated obliquely behind your right ear as you move your clenched left hand to your left hip.

Step forward upon your bent right leg and twist your bent right arm quickly forward and inward so that it contacts the little-finger edge of his left wrist with the little-finger edge of your right wrist.

As soon as you perform the blocking action unclench your right hand but ensure that the fingers are pressed closely together with the thumb also pressed closely against the index finger. Flick your right hand above your left shoulder then extend your right arm as you feign to strike the right side of your partner's neck with the little-finger edge of your right hand. Move your right hand, in the form of a fist, back to your right hip as you make a strong horizontal punching action with your left fist as though to strike his chest.

Try out the actions by defending yourself against your

partner when he attempts to punch your chest with his right fist. He ought to take up the left side stance of Downward Block with his left leg and arm in advance while you stand facing him in a relaxed, natural posture. He moves forward upon his bent right leg and aims his right fist at your breast-bone. You immediately step forward upon your bent left leg as you upraise your bent left arm in order that your left fist is positioned diagonally behind your left ear with palm outwards. When your partner tries to punch you in the chest swing your bent left arm forward so that the little finger of your left wrist is brought into contact with his right wrist and you propel his right arm inwards. Concurrently form your right hand into a fist and move it, palm uppermost, to your right hip.

Unclench your left hand while ensuring that the fingers and thumb are pressed closely together, then move your hand over your right shoulder. Extend your left arm as you swiftly swing the little-finger edge of your left hand forward at the left side of his neck. After you have supposedly struck his neck retract your left hand, in the form of a fist, to your left hip in the prescribed way as you punch powerfully forward with your right fist aimed at his chest (Plate 8).

Now let's consider the compound technique when you are advancing. Your partner should start with the left side stance of Downward Block. He then gets ready to withdraw his left leg and to punch with his right fist as he bends his right leg when it becomes advanced and retracts his left fist to his left hip. He continues by withdrawing his right leg and punching forward with his left fist as he withdraws his right fist to his right hip and his change of position becomes completed. The third punching action is made with his right fist as his right leg becomes advanced.

You ought to stand facing your partner and prepare to advance upon your bent left leg as your partner aims his right fist at your chest. Upraise your bent left arm so that your left fist is positioned behind your left ear. Step forward upon your bent left leg as you swing your bent left arm forward and slightly downwards in such a way that the little-finger edge of your left wrist contacts his right wrist. Still the movement of your left fist as it comes in front of your left shoulder and move your right fist, with palm uppermost, to your right hip. Unclench your left hand as you move it over your right shoulder and then flick your left hand forward and make as if to strike the left side of his neck with the little-finger edge of your left hand. Move your left hand back to your left hip, in the form of a fist, as you punch powerfully forward with your right fist toward your partner's chest.

Your partner continues retreating by moving his right leg backward and prepares to punch forward with his left fist. Extend your left arm horizontally forward as you move your bent right arm upwards so that your right fist is held aloft behind your right ear. Step forward upon your bent right leg as you knock his left wrist inwards with your right wrist and return your left fist to your left hip. Open your right hand and move it over your left shoulder before extending your right arm as you swiftly move the little finger edge of your right hand towards the right side of his neck. Move your right hand back to your right hip, as a fist, as you punch strongly forward with your left fist.

Your partner completes his third step by moving his left leg backwards as he punches forward with his right fist. Move your left fist to the point diagonally behind your left ear and then step forward upon your bent left leg. Make the blocking action by swinging your left arm forward so that your left wrist connects with his right wrist as you retract your right fist to your right hip. Move your left hand over your right shoulder, as you unclench it, then flick your lower arm forward so that you could bring the little-finger edge of your left hand into contact with the left side of his neck. Return your left hand to your left hip in the form of a fist as you punch powerfully forward with your right fist.

Now utilise the defensive and counter actions while you are retreating and your partner is advancing.

Your partner should step forward upon his bent left leg as he tries to punch you in the chest with his left fist. You move your left leg back as you position your right fist diagonally behind your right ear and extend your left arm forward. Bend your right leg while swinging your bent right arm forward so that your right wrist connects with his left wrist and simultaneously withdraw your left fist to your left hip. You swiftly move your unclenched right hand towards the right side of his neck. After seemingly striking your partner's neck you clench your right hand before returning it to your right hip and concurrently punch powerfully forward with your left fist.

As your partner steps forward upon his bent right leg and aims a punch at your chest with his right fist begin to retreat another step. Take back your right leg and upraise your bent left arm with your left fist near to your left ear as you extend your right arm forward. Swing your bent left arm forward so that you contact his right wrist with your left wrist and impel his left arm inwards while withdrawing your right fist to your right hip. Unclench your left hand as you move it to a point over your right shoulder and then flick it forward so that you almost strike the left side of your partner's neck with the little-finger edge of your hand. Return your left hand, as a fist, to your left hip and punch forcefully forward with your right fist toward your partner's chest.

Your partner completes his actions by stepping forward upon his bent left leg as he aims his left fist at your chest. Take back your left leg and upraise your bent right arm in the usual manner as you extend your left arm forward before swinging your right arm forward in order that your right wrist connects with his left wrist and knocks his arm inwards. Move your left hand, as a fist, back to your left hip.

Open your right hand and then move it over your left shoulder preparatory to striking at the right side of his neck with the little-finger edge of your right hand. Return your right hand, in the form of a fist, to your right hip as you punch speedily forward with your left fist.

I recommend that you both go back and forth across your practice area while implementing your respective actions until you can accomplish them smoothly and effectively. The training of the mind in issuing the many messages to the limbs is ideal for getting used to becoming adept at defending yourself against a physical assault. The timing, positioning and distancing can only become mastered by practical application.

Three blocking actions—coupled with counter-punch

A few words of caution. The realistic application of this particular compound blocking action by the defender entails quick and powerful actions. In continuous practice this can result in bruising if movements are slightly uncontrolled or padding is not worn.

You are taken to be in a confined space, such as a corner, when the attacker aims a right-handed punch to your face immediately followed by a left-handed punch to the middle of your body and finally a right-handed punch to your stomach region.

Your partner should aim the three punches at you from the stationary position, of all which you block with one arm and then make a counter-punch with your other arm.

Both you and your partner should face each other before taking up the left side stance of Downward Block. Adjust your positions if required so that you are only just arm's length apart from each other with feet fairly close together.

Your partner starts his moves by aiming his right fist at your nose while retracting his left fist back to his left hip. Move your left fist towards your left hip, palm uppermost, then punch diagonally upwards to your right as you twist your fist so that the knuckles become turned toward you. As you perform Rising Block the little-finger edge of your left wrist impels your partner's right wrist upwards and so prevents his right fist from hitting your face.

Without a pause your partner pulls back his right fist to his right hip, with palm uppermost, as he punches forward with his left fist aimed at your chest. You must quickly move your left arm from the position of Rising Block to Twisting Outside Block (chest level) with the modification that instead of contacting the outside of his wrist as outlined earlier you contact the inside. Achieve this variant of Outside Block by moving your left fist downward then outward before twisting your left fist as you sharply contact the inside of his left wrist with the little-finger edge of your left wrist to propel his lower left arm outwards (Fig. 83).

Your partner speedily retracts his left fist to his left hip while launching his right fist at your stomach. You move your left fist, at great speed, in a downward and inward twisting action so that you knock aside his right wrist by contacting the inside of his wrist with the little-finger edge of your left wrist. Your left wrist is finally moved toward your left hip as you complete this last blocking action with the variant of left side Downward Block.

As you complete the last blocking action make a strong horizontal punch with your right fist at your partner's chest. Stop the movement of your right fist just as it reaches his chest and move your left fist back to your left hip.

FIG. 83

After practising the blocking actions with your left arm switch to using your right arm.

Both you and your partner should take up the position of the right side version of Downward Block with your bent right leg in advance. Vary your positions if necessary so that you are exactly arm's length apart. Your partner should aim his left fist at your nose. You counter this by using your right arm to execute Rising Block so that you knock his left wrist upwards with the little-finger edge of your right wrist. He returns his left fist to his left hip while punching forward with his right fist at your chest. To counter him in turn you quickly move your right fist downward from the position of Rising Block before twisting it outward and then inward so that you dash the little-finger edge of your right wrist into contact with the inside part of his right wrist. He moves his right fist back to his right hip and aims his left fist at your stomach. You speedily twist your right fist downward and inward so that it moves toward the right side of your stomach as you perform the variant of Downward Block. Punch forward with your left fist to your partner's chest.

Avoiding a lunging kick—coupled with counter-punch

In this form of defence the emphasis is placed on the ability to avoid the attacker's lunging kick at your stomach when he rushes at you while lashing out with his foot. Rather than using a blocking action you utilise his forward momentum to brush his leg aside before jabbing a short-range counter-punch into his face or body as he continues to move forward under his own momentum.

You should stand facing your partner at some two full length paces apart. He should prepare to dart forward upon his left bent leg before lashing out with his right foot aimed at your stomach. For the sake of realism he must not hold back but instead allow his onward rush to continue until he becomes able to replace his right foot on the floor when you have successfully steered his foot past your right side.

When your partner begins to lash out with his right foot

FIG. 84

at your stomach step diagonally sideways to your left on
to your bent left leg while forming your hands into fists.
Swing your left fist inwards to your right so that the inside
fleshy part of your lower left arm contacts his right calf
and you thus assist his right foot past your front side
(Fig. 84). Move your right fist to your right hip and then
make a short punch with your right fist near to your partner's face. When you make this punch make sure that you
tense your whole body so that you could deliver a heavy
blow.

Take great care, when practising this defence, that you
do not unintentionally punch your partner in the face. This
danger is prone to happen because of his uncontrolled forward movement which is required for realism. In serious
circumstances the contrary force of the attacker's forward
movement coupled with your punching action greatly increase the effect of your blow.

After you have practised eluding your partner's right

foot get used to dodging his left foot. Stand facing each other just over six feet apart. Your partner should get ready to jump upon his bent right leg prior to lashing out with his left foot aimed at your stomach. Step diagonally outwards upon your bent right leg as you form your hands into fists. Swing your right arm inwards in order that your right forearm comes into contact with his left calf and you thus become able to scoop his lower left leg and foot past your left side. Move your left hand to your left hip and then make a short sharp punch toward his face with your left fist.

You can gain a most useful training in avoiding a rush attack involving a kick. Ask your partner to stand some five paces away before walking quickly toward you. At a predetermined mark or spot some two paces away he should suddenly quicken his movement before launching a kick at your stomach. It will be necessary for you to agree upon the foot he uses during the initial stages of training. It is worth noting that more often than not the attacker will probably use his right foot with which to kick.

Blocking a kick—coupled with counter-punch

While it is essential for training purposes to practise blocking kicks there is a risk of bruising the lower part of your partner's leg during continuous blocking. If he 'pads up' when acting the role of the attacker he will avoid the irksome bruises which might otherwise result. Unfortunately, it is not practical to skim over these awkward blocking actions without loss of an important part of your skill in defence.

The attacker kicks out at your stomach but does not commit his balance as he did in the defensive move just outlined. In this event you cannot successfully guide his foot past your side but must instead rely on Downward Block to knock his leg aside. Stand opposite your partner some two paces apart with loosely clenched hands by your sides.

He should adopt the left side stance of Downward Block with his bent left leg in advance of his right leg. He ought

165

to get ready to bend his right leg before kicking out with his right foot at your stomach.

You counter your partner by making a strong Downward Block with your left arm as you step backward with your right leg and bend your left leg. The little-finger edge of your left wrist must contact the inside part of his lower right leg so that you knock his leg aside. Immediately punch powerfully forward with your right fist toward your part-

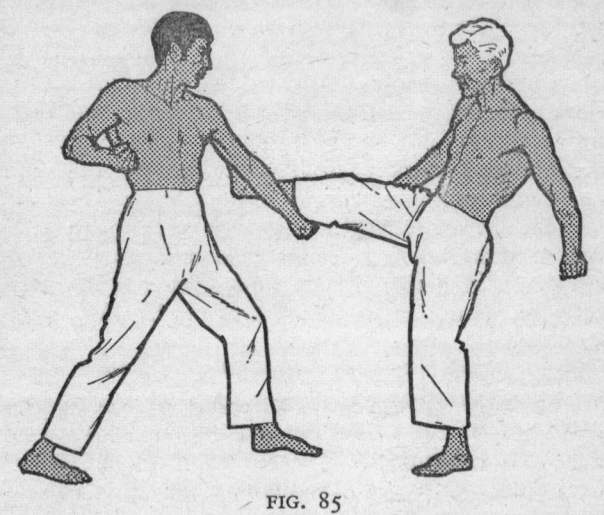

FIG. 85

ner's chest as you swiftly retract your left fist to your left hip (Fig. 85).

After many separate kicking actions with his right foot your partner should kick out with his left foot at your stomach. You are still able to use your left arm to knock his leg aside—the only difference being that you contact the outside of his left leg with the little-finger edge of your left wrist.

While you can generally use your left arm in Downward Block to deflect a kick aimed with either the attacker's left or right leg it is wise also to use your right arm. This is in preparation for the time when it might not be convenient to use your left arm for some reason.

A very useful form of training is gained in defending yourself against a kicking action if your partner stands directly behind you before aiming a kick at your back. During the early stages of training he must call out something like 'now' so that you are warned when he intends to kick out. If under attack from the rear you would have either to hear, or sense, an attack from this quarter and immediately turn about to face the attacker.

The object is to spin round to your left to face your partner while using your left arm in Downward Block to knock aside his oncoming foot. Immediately make a strong forward-punching action with your right hand. You will find at first that you will tend to wobble instead of having a strongly balanced stance, concentrated upon your bent left leg, immediately that you twist about to face your partner. If you make a definite step backwards with your left leg and focus your attention on your left leg, as well as the blocking action, you will quickly be able to stabilise your shift in position.

I have found it a useful form of defence sometimes to dodge kicks by jumping to one side or back before quickly responding with a counter-blow. If you decide to practise dodging kicks aimed at you by your partner be very careful in the initial stages until you become well versed in avoiding his foot.

Three stages of defence against tripping

When you are adopting the recommended stance of the left side version of Downward Block the attacker may attempt to reap your left leg from under you. Such an attacker may use this gambit in order to pierce a formidable defensive stance. He can try to achieve this by bringing the sole of his right foot against the outside of your left ankle—which is somewhat exposed since it is in advance.

Take up the left side style of Downward Block with bent left leg in advance. You should ensure that your left knee is vertical to the toes of your left foot and your back kept straight.

Ask your partner to gently bring the sole of his right foot into contact with the outside of your left ankle. You resist this gentle reaping action by pressing the sole of your left foot firmly into the surface while keeping your left leg bent. Your partner can gradually increase the speed of his reaping action but he must be careful to use the sole of his foot by keeping the little toe nearest the surface, as otherwise unnecessary bruising of your ankle will occur.

2ND DEFENCE

The following form of defence is aptly used when the attacker manages to make you stumble when he brings the sole of his right foot into contact with your left ankle. Request your partner to reap with his right foot against your left ankle. As his reasonably powerful sweeping action takes effect stumble forward into him. Once you are at close quarters make as if to punch him about the chest with your clenched fists. You both take the greatest care, of course, that you do not cause hurt to one another during training.

3RD DEFENCE

In this last-ditch defence, as it were, the attacker is assumed to have managed to knock your leg from under you and caused you to fall to the surface. Even at this seemingly grave disadvantage you are still able to deal him a decisive counter-blow.

Again adopt the left side version of Downward Block with bent left leg in advance while your partner also assumes this stance before closing with you. He should slowly reap your left leg from under you and you should

FIG. 86

gently recline to the floor on to your left flank and left forearm. Bend your right leg and then slowly straighten your
right leg as you raise your right side so that the sole of your
right foot lightly brushes against your partner's stomach
(Fig. 86).

During training it is not requisite to keep falling to the
floor but sufficient to get proficient in the kicking action
from the lying position.

In serious circumstances you can deliver a very effective
kick from the ground against the standing attacker before
he has a chance to kick out at you.

'Chop' to neck

Blows delivered with the edge to the hand receive rather
unfortunate coverage in films and television because of their
spectacular and seemingly deadly effect. There is no doubt
that this blow appeals to some hooligans who wish perhaps
to enlarge their limited, but potentially dangerous, fighting
ability. Fortunately the appeal of this form of blow will

probably diminish once it becomes hackneyed through constant use on film.

Let's assume that your partner will attempt to bring the little-finger edge of his right hand into contact with the left side of your neck. You must block his arm with the little-finger edge of your left wrist. Move your left hand near to your right ear with palm inwards as you straighten your right arm forward. Move your unclenched left hand for-

FIG. 87

ward and slightly downward so that you use the little-finger edge of your left wrist to baulk his right wrist in order to prevent the edge of his right hand from hitting your neck. Return your clenched right hand to your chest. Grip his right wrist with your left hand in such a way that the thumb of your hand presses against the back of his wrist. Twist the knuckles of your left hand forward while twisting his wrist so that he becomes awkwardly twisted over the outside edge of his right foot.

Once you have twisted his arm keep your balance by adopting a forward stance upon your bent left leg as you

deliver a front kick with your right foot to his stomach or
chest (Fig. 87).

In action you may find yourself a trifle too near the
attacker to deliver the kick. All you need do to rectify the
distancing is quickly to move your left foot back as you
launch your right foot at the middle of his body.

After you have become used to blocking your partner's
right hand practise blocking his left hand. Straighten your
left arm forward and move your unclenched right hand to
near your left ear. As your partner tries to strike the right
side of your neck with his left arm make Knife-edge Block
with your right wrist as you withdraw your opened left
hand to your chest. Grip his left wrist with your right hand
and twist his arm as you adopt forward stance with your
right leg allowed to become bent. Deliver a kick to the
middle of his body with your left foot.

As always you should try out the complete counter nu-
merous times.

Defence against Holds in
Standing Position

There is a clear distinction in the circumstance when one
should utilise one of the following counters and when a
word or two will suffice to free you from a hold. In a prank
no harm is done, of course, if you do not retaliate physically.
On the other hand in a situation involving a stranger, where
you are in physical danger, it is a different matter and it
is the latter possibility that is catered for here. It is a matter of sound judgement to use the barest minimum amount
of force against an assailant thought necessary to safeguard
yourself from serious injury.

Grip on wrist
Let's assume that the attacker, who is standing facing you,
tightly grips your left wrist with his right hand. Stand with

FIG. 88

your feet about shoulder width apart so that you have a
reasonably strongly balanced posture and ask your partner
to hold your wrist with his hand. Clench your hands and
move the palm of your right fist upwards to near your left
ear so that the knuckles of your fist are outwards.

Now make a variant of Downward Block with your
right arm. Snap your right arm downwards so that the
little-finger edge of your right wrist connects forcibly with
his right wrist as you impart a powerful turning action of
your shoulders to your right (Fig. 88). As this action impels
his right wrist inwards it will have the effect of causing his
body to become twisted so that his back could be turned
to you. Retract your freed left fist to your left hip, then use
your left fist to punch forward so that you could strike him
in the region of his ribs dependent upon the degree to which
his body has become twisted (Fig. 89).

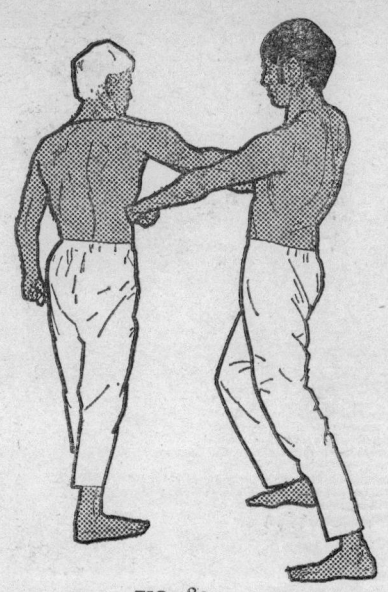

FIG. 89

After you have gained experience of disrupting the grip on your left wrist try out the same form of counter when your partner grips your right wrist with his left hand. In this event you move your clenched left fist to near your right ear before performing a similar movement to Downward Block and then make the punching action with your right fist.

If the attacker holds both your wrists from the front you should deal him a blow with either your knee or foot dependent upon the distance separating you from him. When you deliver your counter-blow it is best to move your wrists towards your hips so that the attacker is pulled toward you to increase the effectiveness of your counter.

If the attacker approaches you from behind before grasping your wrists at the sides of your body bow forward from the waist as you draw your wrists toward your stomach and lash out backwards with your feet in a flurry of blows at the attacker's shins and body.

If the attacker approaches from the side and grasps your wrist with both hands twist towards him and use your unencumbered elbow to hit his ribs or face. If necessary supplement this with a blow from your knee.

Overarm grip from behind

In this example the presumption is that the attacker unexpectedly clamps your arms against your sides from behind by enveloping your arms and body with his arms. It is a mistake to attempt wriggling your arms free. If the attacker is of approximately the same strength or of greater strength it is difficult quickly to escape and this is particularly vital if you are being held by one assailant while another advances toward you.

Ask your partner to clamp your arms against your sides by hugging you from behind. Well bend your right leg and raise it into the air as you turn the toes of your right foot directly outwards to your right. Contact his right leg just below his right knee with the outside edge of your right foot then move the outside edge of your foot downward against his shin so that you could scrape it painfully downwards. As your right foot nears his right instep make as if to stamp downward with the sole of your foot. In serious circumstances your actions are, of course, speeded up and if you happen to be wearing shoes the stamping action is very telling upon the attacker.

As soon as you have used your right foot replace it on the surface. While you are not able to move your upper body and upper arms you are still able to move your legs and lower arms to a limited degree.

Skip a few inches to your left on your left foot followed by your right foot. By this action you will have exposed the attacker's middle body to a 'cut' with the edge of your right hand. Bow well forward from the waist as you straighten your right arm forward with unclenched hand in advance and fingers pressed closely together (Fig. 90). Swing your

FIG. 90

right hand backwards and upwards between his legs so that
you could deliver a painful blow with the little-finger edge
of your right hand.

There is little doubt that the stamping action combined
with the edge of hand blow would tend to loosen the
attacker's grip upon your body to a marked degree. Dependent upon the opportunities you could then effectively
use your elbows to knock him backwards away from you
followed by a backward kick.

There are two other important facets of this defence to
consider. As I observed the attacker may have an accom-
plice who advances from the front.

If you are held from behind in the standing position,
while another potential attacker closes with you, it is best
to deal with the one in front at first since the other's arms
are engaged in holding you. Use your right foot powerfully to kick the advancing attacker in the knee or stomach

with your right foot. Immediately you have dealt with the man in front use the counters previously described for the one who is restraining you.

The second variant of this form of attack is when the attacker attempts to lift you bodily from the ground before hurling you back to the surface. You can foil his aim, irrespective of his strength, by entwining your right foot around the lower part of his right leg. As he violently jerks you up in the air allow your right foot to slide up his right leg. When he has reached the unexpected extent of his lift he will be constrained to lower you back to the surface. You can smash your elbows backwards into the attacker when you are in the air and use the other counters when he lowers you feet first to the ground.

Grip on sleeve

The attacker may grasp your right sleeve with his left hand before pulling you toward him as he lashes out with his right fist. By using this type of contrary movement there is little doubt that the effective power of the attacker's punch would be greatly enhanced.

Alternately you may attempt a retaliatory punch against the attacker with your right fist which he manages to prevent from hitting his body and at the same time succeeds in grasping your sleeve.

Stand facing your partner at a distance of one large pace apart. Make a slow punching action with your right fist as you step forward upon your bent right leg. Ask your partner to knock your arm downwards as he clasps your sleeve with his left hand.

Forcefully bend your right arm by swinging your right fist in a large counter-clockwise action so that it traverses the front of your body, from right to left, to above your left shoulder. At the same time withdraw your right leg a trifle so that you use the power of your body quickly to wrench your right arm to your left and free it from the hindrance of his grip upon your sleeve. Continue the large counter-clockwise movement of your right fist by raising it above your head before swinging it downward so that you could use the little-finger edge of your fist to strike his left collar-bone as you tense your stomach muscles. This is the so-called hammer blow. It is important that you train many times so that you incorporate the power of your body when you retract your right arm and leg to disrupt his grip upon your sleeve. Substitute left for right where required so that you get used to freeing your left arm from the encumbrance of a grip upon your left sleeve.

Grip on hair from behind

You can be placed in a very dangerous predicament if the attacker approaches from behind your back in the standing position and grasps you by the hair or collar before pulling you backwards to the ground into the sitting position. If he succeeds in tugging you backwards to the ground you would be in the unenviable position of sitting upon the surface with your back turned fully to him while he is still standing. It hardly bears contemplating what devastating effect any further attacks which he might care to launch could then have upon you.

Request your partner to stand behind you before grasping your hair with his right hand. As soon as your partner grasps your hair and begins to pull you backwards upraise your hands and tightly grip his right wrist with both of your hands. Clamp his hand against your head so that he cannot wrench your hair.

Your next object is to correct your weak posture of being bent over uncomfortably backwards by being curved powerfully forward. Accomplish this change in posture by running backwards past your partner's right side while still maintaining a firm hold upon his right wrist. By your purposeful actions you will have managed to twist his right arm awkwardly backwards while getting somewhat behind his right side. Straighten your body a little as you add to the awkwardness of his position by raising his wrist upwards in such a way that the palm of his right hand is kept uppermost.

FIG 91

Support your weight on your slightly bent left leg so that you could tap him on the chest with the ball of your right foot, or toe cap if you are wearing outdoor footwear (Fig. 91).

It does not materially matter if the attacker uses his left hand or both hands to grip your hair, or even the back of your collar. Still run backwards past his right side while maintaining a firm hold upon his wrist or wrists. This will have the effect of twisting his body toward you which will expose him even more to your counter-attack.

Grip on hair from front

In this illustration the presumption is that the attacker is facing you and tightly grasps your hair with his right hand. Such an attacker may well use his grip upon your hair to pull you forcefully forward and downward with the intention of jabbing his knee into your face. The effect of such a savage blow would undoubtedly disable even the most robust amongst us and this attack is therefore very dangerous.

If you are caught totally unawares the best negative

form of defence is literally to charge forward while pushing your head into his stomach and to protect your face with your forearms. The effect of your onward rush will knock him backwards and he would not be able to stabilise his posture enough to dash his knee against your face.

Let us now consider a defence when you have a split second warning of the impending attack. Stand facing your partner and ask him to grasp your hair with his right hand. Quickly raise your hands and tightly clasp his right wrist in such a way that your thumbs press against the pulse side of his wrist in what is termed an alternate thumb grip. Keep your hands almost stationary as you withdraw your right leg and side so that the attacker's right arm becomes reasonably straight. Move your left elbow over his right arm so that his arm becomes positioned under your left armpit. Continue turning to your right while keeping close to your partner's right side. Clamp your left elbow against your left side so that his right arm becomes firmly nipped between your chest and the inside of your left lower arm as you turn to face the same direction to which he is facing while standing close to his right side.

You are now in a position to create a bone lock upon your partner's right arm. This is brought about by ensuring that the thumb of his right hand is made to point downwards as you move his wrist upwards while leaning to your left so that you bear oppressively downwards upon his upper arm with the left side of your chest and armpit. Finalise your actions by maintaining your balance upon your bent right leg as you make a 'Back heel' Kick with your left heel so that you could rap your partner's jaw with your left heel.

In really dire circumstances you could make the kicking action as you bear downwards the attacker's upper arm so that a contrary action is utilised to add power to your actions.

Get your partner to grasp your hair with his left hand and apply the armlock upon his left arm coupled with a backward Kicking action of your right heel (Fig. 92).

FIG. 92

Stranglehold from behind

If an attacker stealthily gets into position behind you he can apply this form of stranglehold. Apart from the obvious danger of being throttled into submission the great problem for a defender to overcome in attacks involving the neck is momentarily to force the mind to put aside the fear, or pain, of being subjected to a stranglehold while delivering an effective counter-attack. This concept really applies to all attacks involving particularly vulnerable parts of the body.

It is very easy for experienced men to think that it is relatively simple to repulse such attacks, as the one we are presently considering, by dealing the attacker blows. This idea ignores the difficulty of those lacking experience to concentrate on the counter instead of the danger to the neck. You can overcome this possibly grave disadvantage by training assiduously so that you become quite used to an attacking movement against your neck. You can also get so adept at using the counters that there is very little chance of the attacker's actions from progressing far enough to create this difficulty.

The usual practical form of applying a stranglehold from behind is for the attacker to slip his hand over your shoulder before lodging his wrist across the front of your throat. He then presses his other forearm against the nape of your neck or head to achieve contrary pressure upon your throat or neck.

Ask your partner to stand in close proximity behind you before passing his right hand over your right shoulder and then across the front of your throat. As his right hand nears the left side of your collar he should insert his thumb inside your collar and obtain a firm hold on your jacket just below your left ear. At the completion of these actions the thumb edge of his right wrist will be pressing into the left side and front of your neck and he ought to move his left forearm upward into contact with the nape of your neck. To apply the stranglehold your partner would now merely have to draw his right elbow backward so that the thumb edge of his right wrist becomes drawn across your throat while he pushes his left forearm against the back of your neck.

Your partner must not apply the stranglehold, under any circumstances, as all such holds are inherently dangerous unless a competent teacher is present to supervise their application.

Once your partner becomes used to going through the motions of correctly applying the stranglehold you are then able to begin to implement the counters.

As your partner gets into position raise your right leg into the air and fully turn your foot outwards to your right. Press the little toe edge of your right foot against his right leg just below his right knee and make as if to scrape your foot down his right shin into his right instep.

After you have made the stamping action with your right foot prepare to smash your left elbow backwards into his chest a couple of times. Clench your left hand to form it into a fist then contort your hips to your left as you make as if to drive your left elbow back into his ribs.

The supposition is that by this stage the attacker will not be holding you as firmly as he may have been to start with and you are therefore able to throw him to the ground. You can begin to accomplish the throwing action by grasping his right sleeve, or right arm, tightly with your hands as you step a small pace outwards upon your bent left leg. You outstretch your right leg to your right with the inside of the foot upon the floor and your knee turned slightly downwards. Now if you tug at your partner's right sleeve as you twist your hips to your left he will revolve about your body and be lightly rolled over your outstretched right leg to the floor.

It is imperative in training that you both take care not to hurt one another by being competitive while using too forceful actions. I think it worth remembering that when we know ourselves to be in any sort of emergency requiring physical action that adrenalin is released and we are capable of unusual motive power for either 'fight or flight'. Provided, therefore, technique is correctly learnt muscular power is always quickly available in an emergency.

Grip under arms from front
If the attacker is proud of his physical prowess he may use a bear-like hug to squeeze your diaphragm. Should his strength equal his confidence he could cause you some pain while attempting to bend you over backwards.

Request your partner to stand in front of you and then to pass his arms under your arms before tightly grasping your body. Tightly clasp each side of his jacket with your hands as you raise your right foot in the air. Turn your right foot outward before contacting his left leg just below his left knee with the inside edge of your foot. Maintaining your grips upon his coat, gently move your right foot down your partner's left shin into his left instep.

Continue your counters by replacing your right foot upon the floor as you quickly move your left knee toward the vicinity of his stomach with the supposed intention of jabbing him with your knee.

After you have replaced your left foot firmly upon the floor release your grips upon his coat and upraise your arms so that your unclenched hands are raised above your head. Bring your arms downwards and thrust the little-finger edges of your hands into each side of his waist in a cutting-like action just above the hip joint and below the first rib.

Raise your right foot from the floor and pass it between his lower legs. Lodge the heel of your right hand under your partner's chin and then use your well placed right leg to reap his left leg forward by contacting the calf of his leg with your right calf. At the same instant gently push your partner's chin upwards so that you press his head backwards. The culmination of these actions will result in your partner slowly reclining backwards to the floor.

In a fight if your individual actions are not entirely effective you would still have the advantage and this is the main reason why I think you should always use more than one form of counter to holds upon your body.

Grip over arms from front
In this type of assault the attacker clamps your elbows tightly against your sides while applying a bear-like hug to squeeze your body.

Since you cannot effectively use your hands at the beginning you must use your foot and knee. Stamp downward with your right foot and make the upward blow with your left knee as just recommended for countering 'Grip under arms from front'. After such treatment the attacker's hold about your arms will at least be loosened and you would thus be in a position to throw him backward with a similar throwing action to that of the technique just described.

Stranglehold from front

If a physically strong man grasps your neck in an attempt to throttle you it can prove to be a very disconcerting and serious form of attack.

The main pre-requisite to bear in mind if you are totally unprepared is that you must move backwards if possible so that the attacker is not permitted to keep his arms bent and thus be able immediately to use his maximum strength upon your neck. Even if your back is against a wall you must keep in motion, even to the side, so that he cannot exert his full strength against you.

It is sometimes best to offer two distinct methods of defence even in basic technique. 'A' method will suit you if you are tall while 'B' method will be convenient if you are not particularly tall.

'A' METHOD

Your partner should stand facing you before lightly gripping your neck with his hands so that his thumbs press gently upon your windpipe. Shuffle backwards then dislodge his grip upon your neck by twisting your head to your left as you swing your right arm upwards and inwards in a large counter-clockwise action.

When you knock his left arm inwards with the inside of your right arm continue your actions by twisting your hips sharply to your left as your unclenched right hand nears your left ear (Fig. 93). Once you have brushed your partner's hands away from your neck twist your hips back to your right as you bring the little-finger edge of your right hand downwards into gentle contact with the right side of his neck.

In a dangerous situation you would have to wrench your head and body to your left to disrupt the hold about your neck. This might even cause some bruising to your neck but this is preferable to having to succumb to the attack.

FIG. 93

'B' METHOD

Once your partner grips your neck start your counter actions
by moving backwards so that his arms become somewhat
extended. Grasp his wrists tightly with both hands and then
prepare to kick him with your right foot. Well bend your
right leg then flick the lower part of your right leg forward
so that you can use the ball of your right foot to contact his
stomach.

As you make this action draw your partner's arms slowly
forward and outward as though you mean to use a powerful
contrary action as an aid to the effectiveness of your kicking
action.

Sometimes it may not be possible to retreat and you
would therefore have to use your knee to strike at the
attacker when he is at close quarters. You should get your
partner to stand fairly close to you while you grip his wrists
as before. Move your right knee in slow motion toward his

stomach as you draw his wrists downward and outward.

In the sort of circumstance just outlined you might have to use your knee to strike the attacker more than once to knock him away.

Should you be in the supine position when an attacker attempts to throttle you the best initial defence is to use your hands to prise his thumbs away from your neck and then violently to twist his thumbs against their joints as you wriggle your body and lash out with your feet or knees.

Defence against a flurry of blows

At one time or another you will, no doubt, have noticed one of the contestants in a boxing match clamp the other participant's arms under his armpits so that the other man cannot momentarily use his fists effectively to strike with. While the referee is quick to admonish a man for this conduct in boxing this type of tactic is useful for you to use in a fight at close quarters if a man attacks you with a hail of punches and kicks.

The idea is to hold his arms, dodge any kick or blow with his knee and to prevent him from using his head to butt your face.

Your partner should close to within a short distance away with his arms positioned in front of him in a sparring position. Quickly grasp his sleeves close to the hollow of his elbow joints and then step forward on your slightly bent left leg to his right side. Your left foot should now be positioned close to the outside of his right foot as you tightly clamp his arms between your arms and sides. Swing your right leg forward between your own left leg and his right leg and position the right side of your face near to his right shoulder. Simultaneously tense your whole body so that he cannot move his arms as you bear oppressively downwards upon him to limit his power of movement.

Suddenly relax your downward pressure, while taking care to maintain your holds upon his sleeves, so that your partner also tends automatically to relax. As soon as you feel that he relaxes this is the opportune moment to throw him slowly to the ground. Accomplish the throwing movement gently by swinging your straightened right leg backwards with toes pointed downwards, so that the back of your right thigh contacts the back of his right thigh. As this slow-motion reaping action takes effect pull your partner upward and then push downward as he falls to the floor.

It is necessary for you to become adroit at catching the attacker's sleeves for this mode of defence. The best way to achieve this facility is for your partner to keep advancing toward you, in a sparring position, while you constantly practise getting a firm grip upon his sleeves. As soon as you achieve your holds dart forward to his right side and make as if to throw him backwards to the floor.

Defence against the Armed Attacker

If the attacker is armed with gun, knife or the notorious 'blunt instrument' of legal jargon you are placed in the worst possible predicament.

While it is perhaps an over simplification to generalise I do not think it sensible to offer the many set unarmed 'defences' against the attacker if he is holding a gun levelled at your chest or back. To my mind all these so-called counters of Karate, Judo or any other form of self-defence which I have seen are not practical and are therefore dangerous ever to rely upon.

A gunman either means to shoot or he does not. If he uses the weapon as a threat it is wise not to attempt to disarm him as this will only precipitate the possibly fateful decision for him to pull the trigger.

While some script writers in the inevitable 'Western' movies imagine the barrel of the gun to be pressed firmly against the 'hero's' back or front, which lends itself to counter, this must be very exceptional in reality. If, as seems more logical, the gunman stands some little distance away with the weapon pointed unwaveringly at you, and his elbow close to his side, then you can be quite certain that he is competent enough to squeeze the trigger.

I think the best tactic to adopt in this unhoped-for predicament is to use mental cunning with a gunman and not to make an attempt to disarm him unless it is vital for the protection of your person or that of others. Should you be faced by no other recourse but to try disarming him you would have to attempt to lull him into a false sense of security before attempting to 'jump him'.

Before we consider a few individual methods of self-protection against the armed attacker, who is not in possession of a firearm, it is important to make some general observations. If you are indoors, where portable pieces of furniture are within reach, you could, of course, quickly grasp a chair or some other article and use this to defend yourself or others with.

If you are out of doors you could use possessions such as an umbrella, walking stick, brief case, book or even loose change in your pocket to protect yourself with. With imagination it is surprising how many exceptional ways one can use these quite ordinary sorts of possessions to hit, baulk or distract the attacker. In this connection it may not be amiss to mention an incident which, I now recall a little shame-facedly, happened when I was a small boy. A famous wrestler was romping with me and he had held me upon the ground and told me it was impossible, even for a small boy, to escape from this particular hold once it was applied. I promptly slipped off my shoe with a free hand and tapped him on the head! Fortunately for me he thought it was quite a trick for a youngster to use and took it in good part although I remember immediately feeling a little guilty about it.

In Karate it is generally accepted that it is best to block the attacker's blows. This would not be the wisest course to adopt if the attacker happens to be holding a knife or indeed any sharp pointed weapon. Even if you block his initial thrust, if he releases his grip by design, or due to the jarring effect of your blocking action, the weapon could dart forward and wound you with the point. Another factor, that is often overlooked, is that if the weapon is inordinately long he may still succeed in wounding you with the point even though you manage to accomplish a blocking action.

There are many spectacular defences offered as a counter to a downward thrust with a knife which call for an initial blocking action, but to my mind this type of attack is mainly fictional. The most formidable knife thrust to contend with is still the one that the ancient Corsican bandit was reputed to have admonished his son to use—'put your thumb on the blade and strike upwards'.

There are two main and basic forms of unarmed defence to consider which both call for an avoiding movement. The attacker may execute a downward blow with a 'blunt instrument' aimed at your head or he may use an upward thrust with a sharp pointed weapon at your stomach.

Downward blow

Your partner should hold a stick in his right hand and prepare to step forward on his right leg as he upraises his right arm before bringing the stick slowly but directly down towards your head.

As your partner swings the stick down towards your head you must skip sideways to your left on to your left foot. Move your unclenched hands in front of your chest, positioning them some twelve inches apart with thumbs nearest you. Ensure that you press the fingers of each hand together before jabbing the little-finger edge of your hands against his arm so that your right hand connects with the outside of his forearm and your left hand connects with the back of his elbow or upper arm. Move your right leg and side back so that you twist to face him as you press his arm forward and downward to guide the stick which he is holding past your front. This completes the vital avoiding and deflecting actions necessary to evade the downward blow (Fig. 94).

Once the attacker's arm has been diverted in this way and the speed of his arm movement has diminished you can

FIG. 94

clutch at his arm or sleeve. You can then swing him face
forward to the ground by sharply pulling his arm forward
and round to your right as you continue to twist to your
right. From his prone position a well-placed blow or two
by you will suffice to preclude any further immediate attack
from him.

If the attacker does not commit his balance too far forward, or if he is comparatively heavy, it may not be easy
to swing him face forward to the ground. In this event provided you momentarily retard his right arm, after avoiding
a possibly more controlled form of blow, you can still deal
him a devastating counter-blow. This means you admin-

ister one or more powerful kicks to his body with your right foot while you use the grips of your hands upon his arm or sleeve to pull him into the blows.

Both you and your partner should gradually increase the speed of your actions but remember for your part that the deflection of his arm is crucial and do not try to grip his sleeve or arm at too early a juncture.

Upward thrust

When the attacker makes a horizontal or upward blow with a knife, or any sharp pointed weapon, toward your stomach you must divert the thrust by knocking his oncoming arm aside as you move to a contrary direction. With the benefit of some sound training in Karate it is probably best to use

FIG. 95

a form of Downward Block for this purpose which utilises a certain degree of an already acquired skill.

Your partner should not use a sharp knife at first. Indeed it is wise and thoughtful if he uses an imitation. He should hold the 'knife' in his right hand and move it slowly toward your stomach. You must skip quickly to your left on to your left leg as you swing your clenched right hand in a counter-clockwise circular action. Strike his right forearm with the little-finger edge of your right wrist at the completion of this circular action so that you could dash his arm away to your right.

You place your weight upon your left leg and then kick forward at his ribs with your right foot while still momentarily keeping your right arm in the original warding-off position (Fig. 95). Deliver a secondary blow with your left fist aimed at his face as you quickly replace your right foot upon the floor.

Complete your actions by gripping his right wrist with your right hand and tug it to your right so that you could snap his right arm across the front of your body and at the very least make him relinquish his grip upon the weapon.